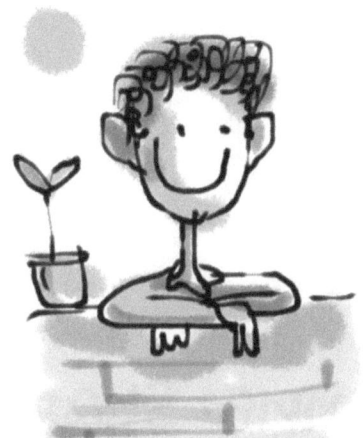

Chapters

1. Simple Shapes.
2. Cute Expressions.
3. Create Your Own Happiness.
4. Finding Happiness in Eveything.
5. Gratitude Doodles.

Simple Shapes

These are common shapes around us.
Find the shapes in everything you
see and draw simple doodles.

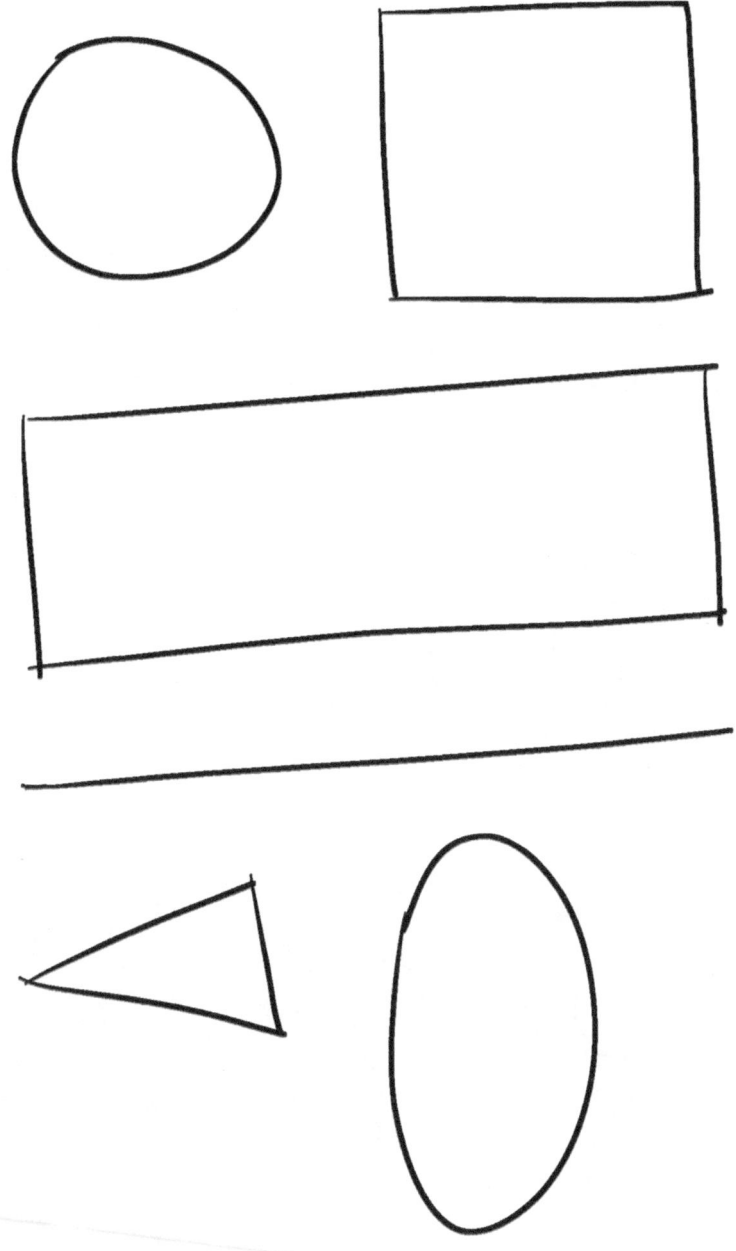

NAME ME

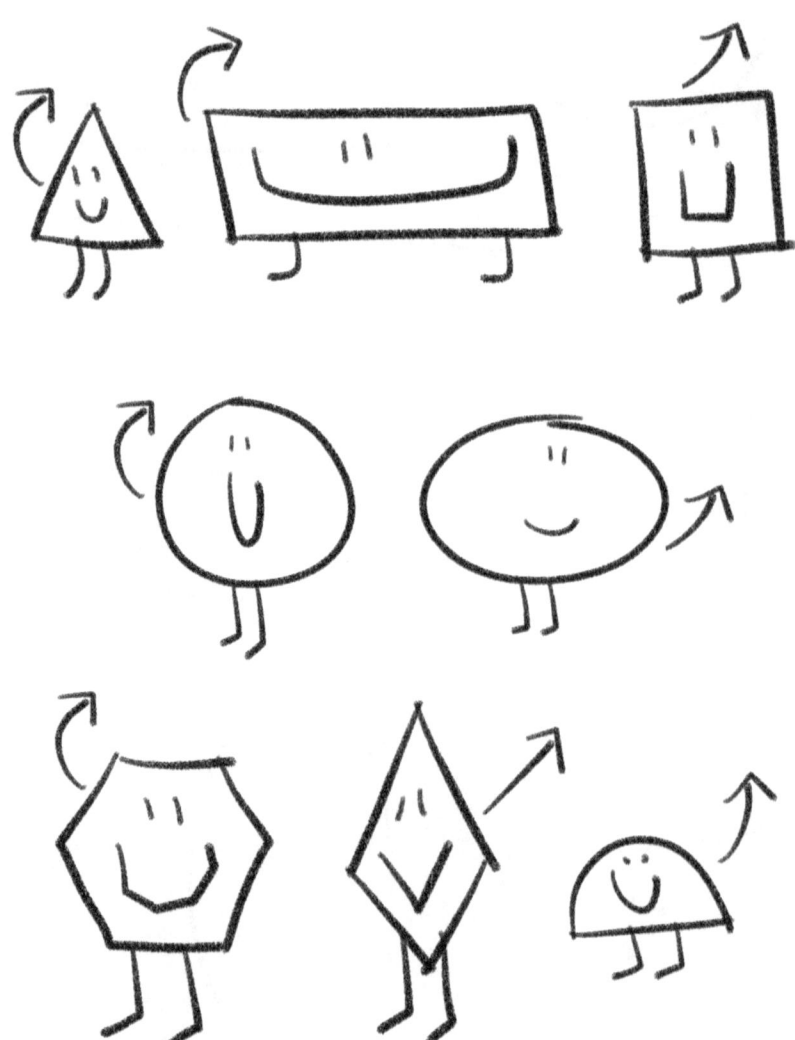

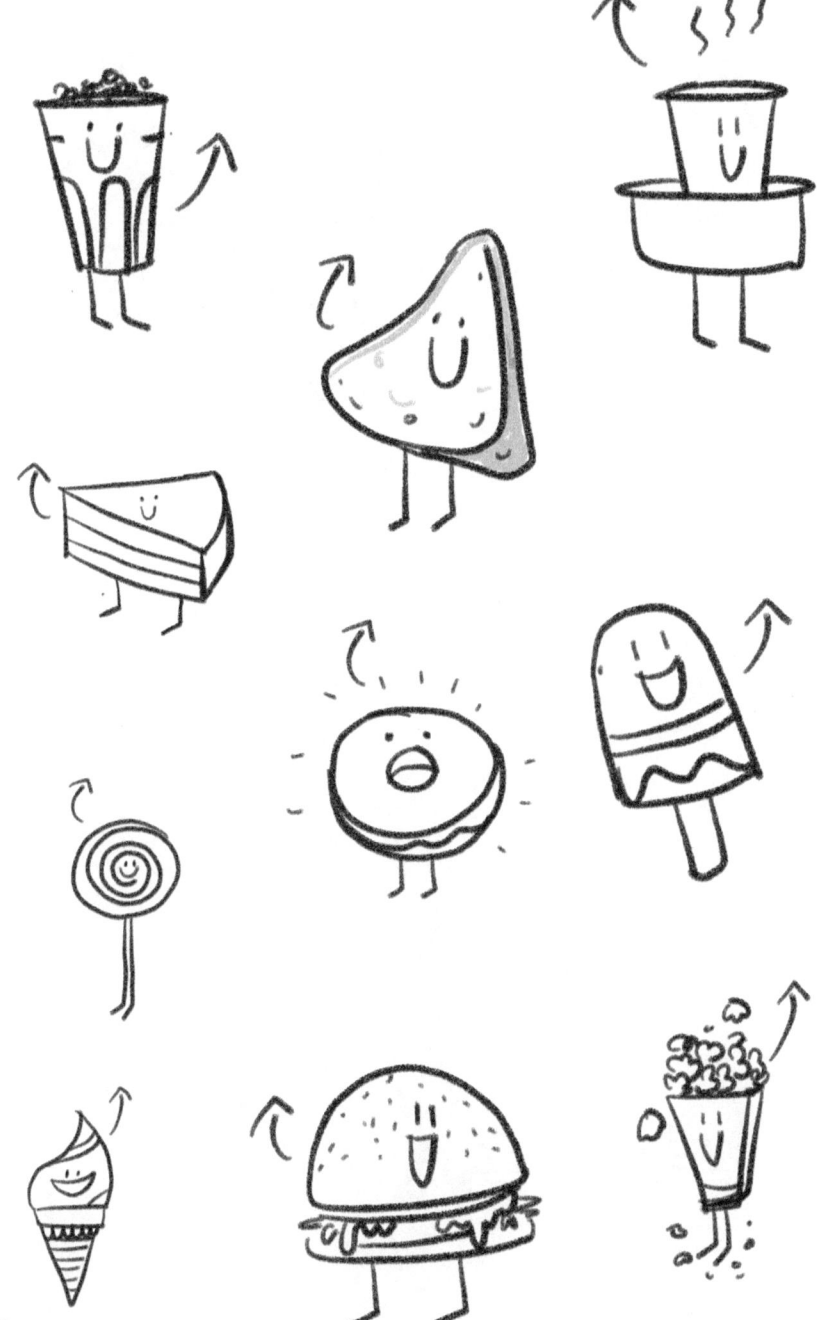

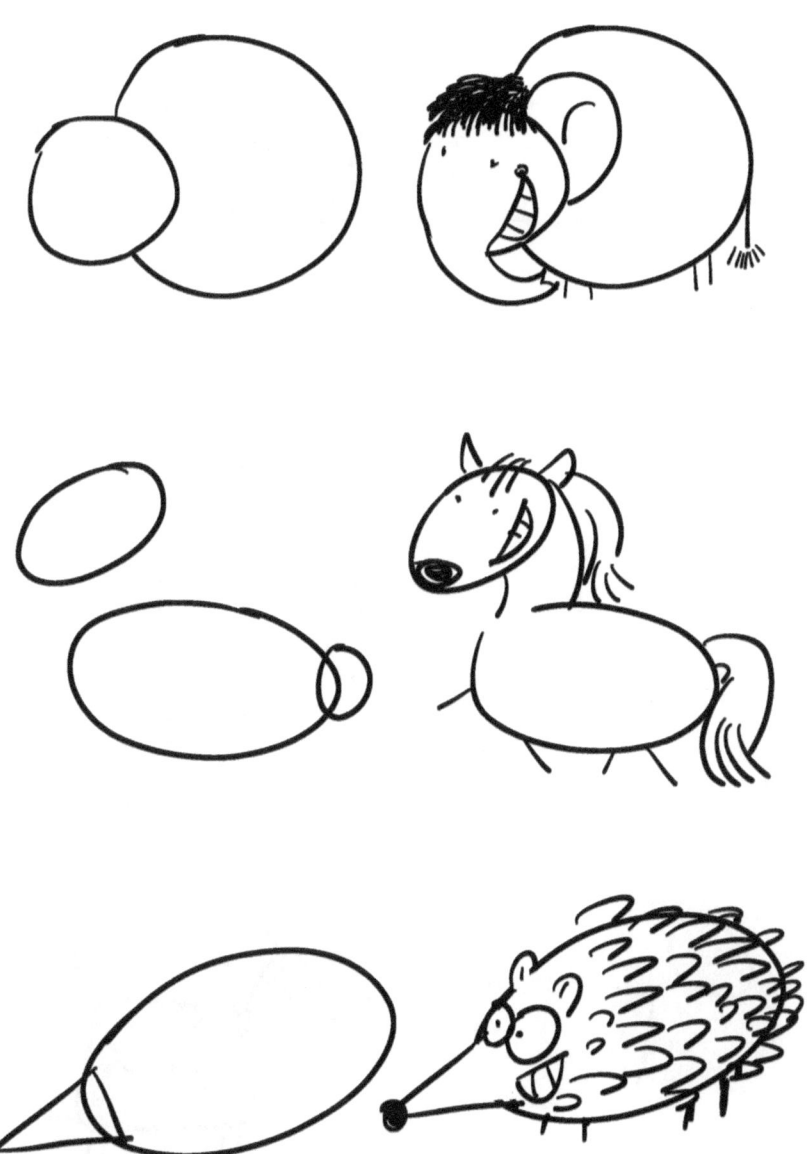

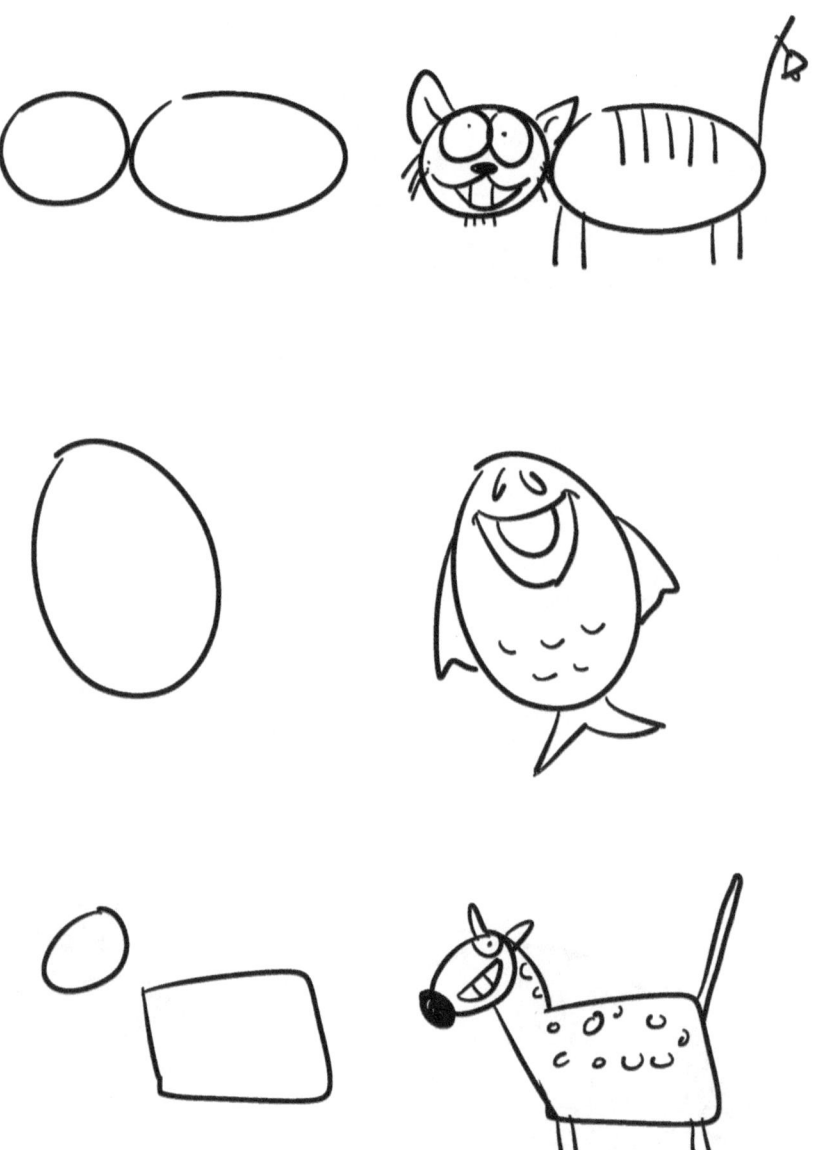

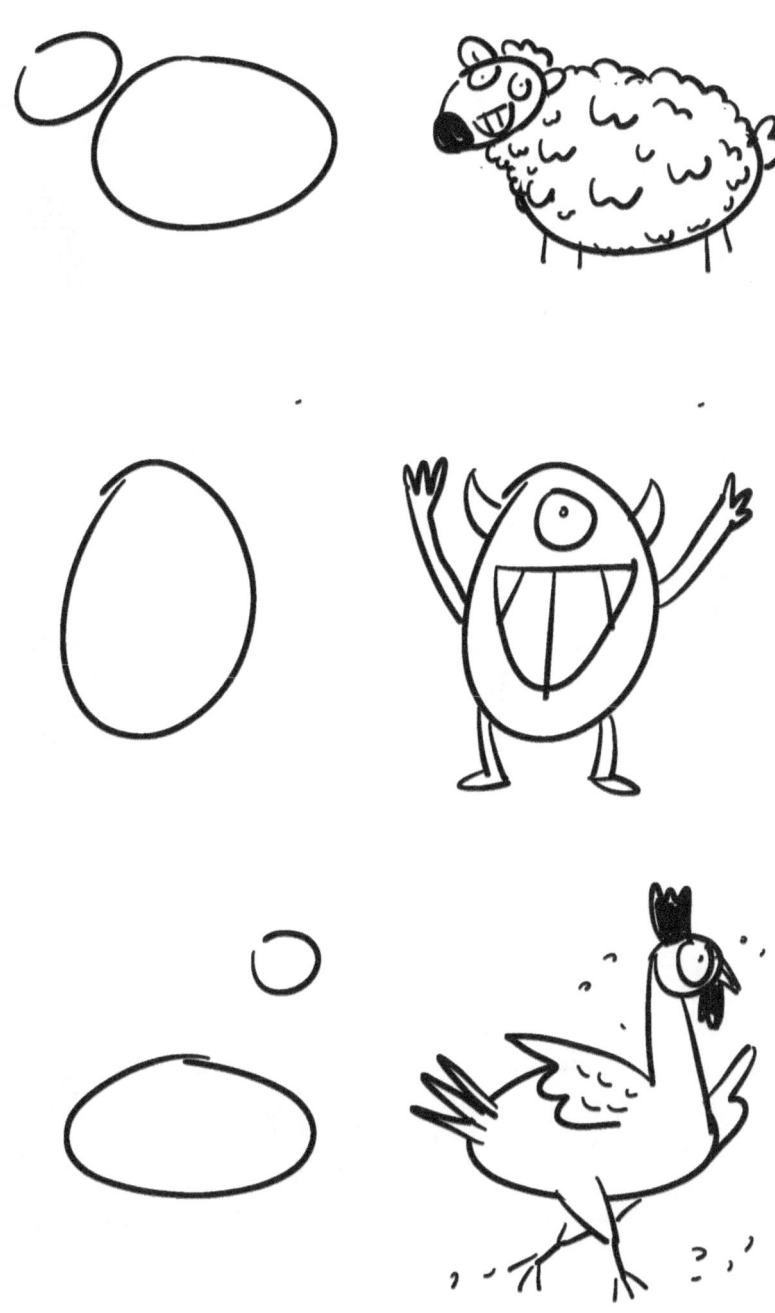

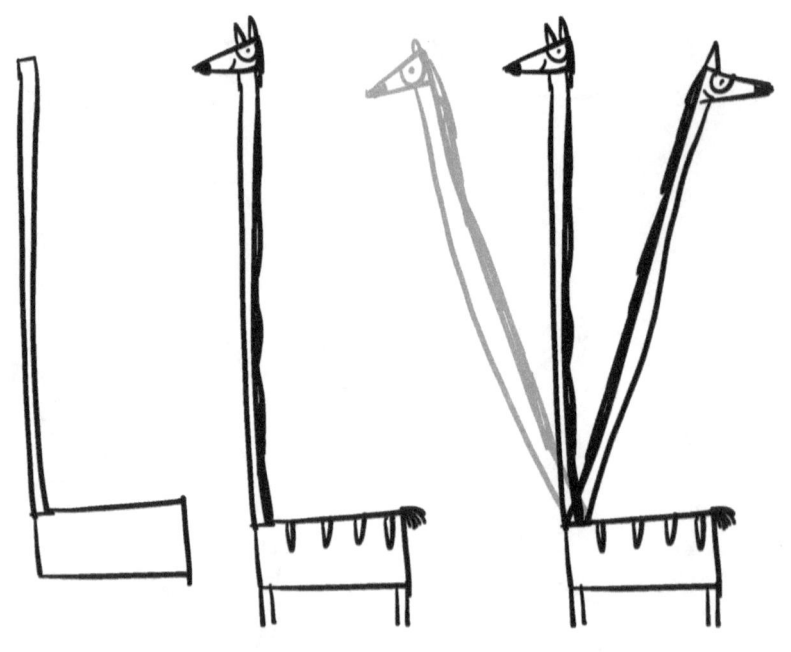
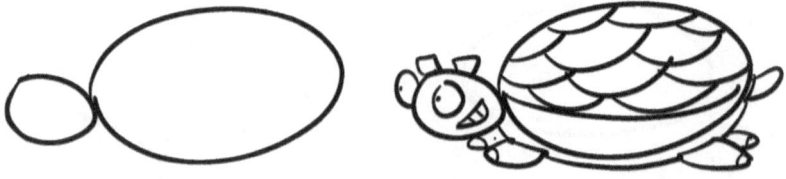

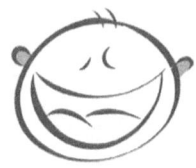

Cute Expressions from Simple Lines

After finishing the first chapter you will be comfortable drawing doodles from different shapes. This chapter allows you to add emotional elements to it. This adds more fun to your doodling experience.

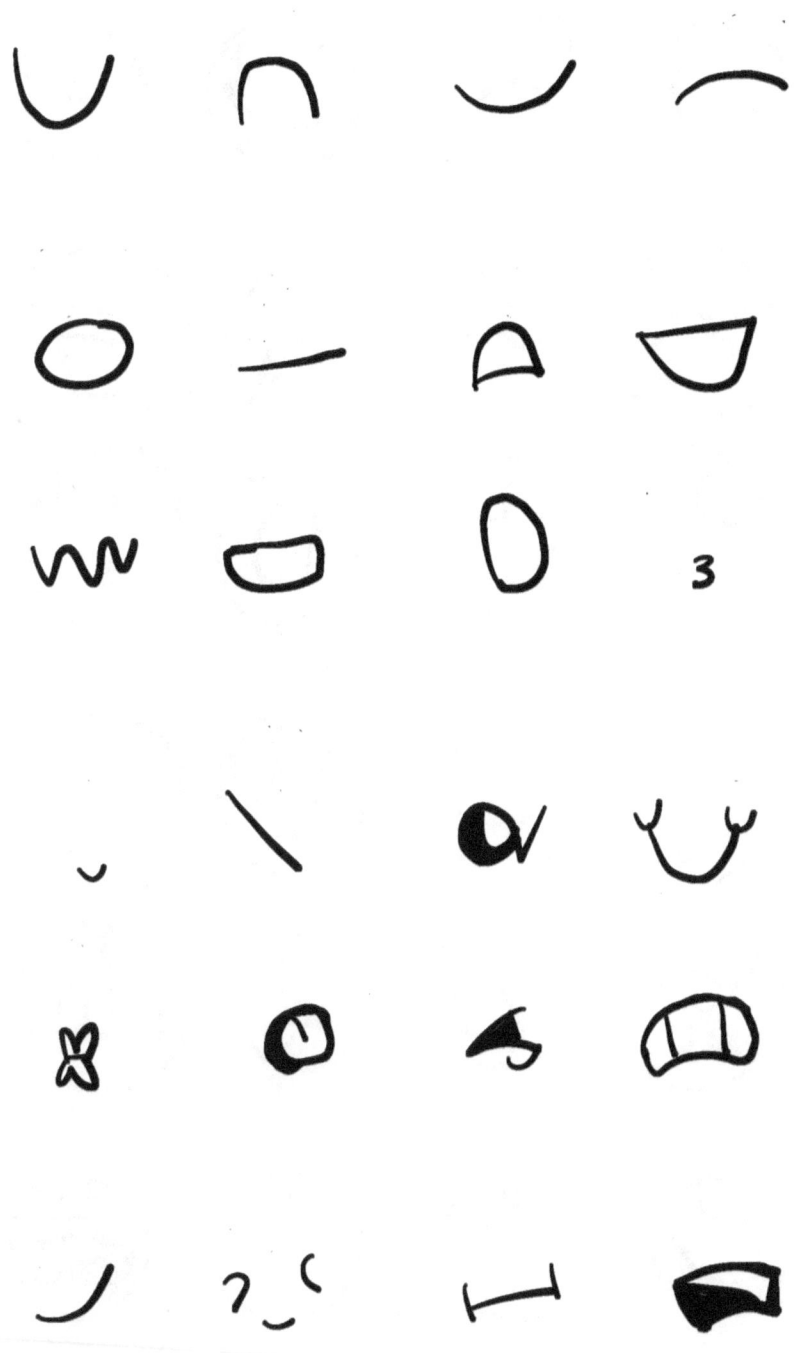

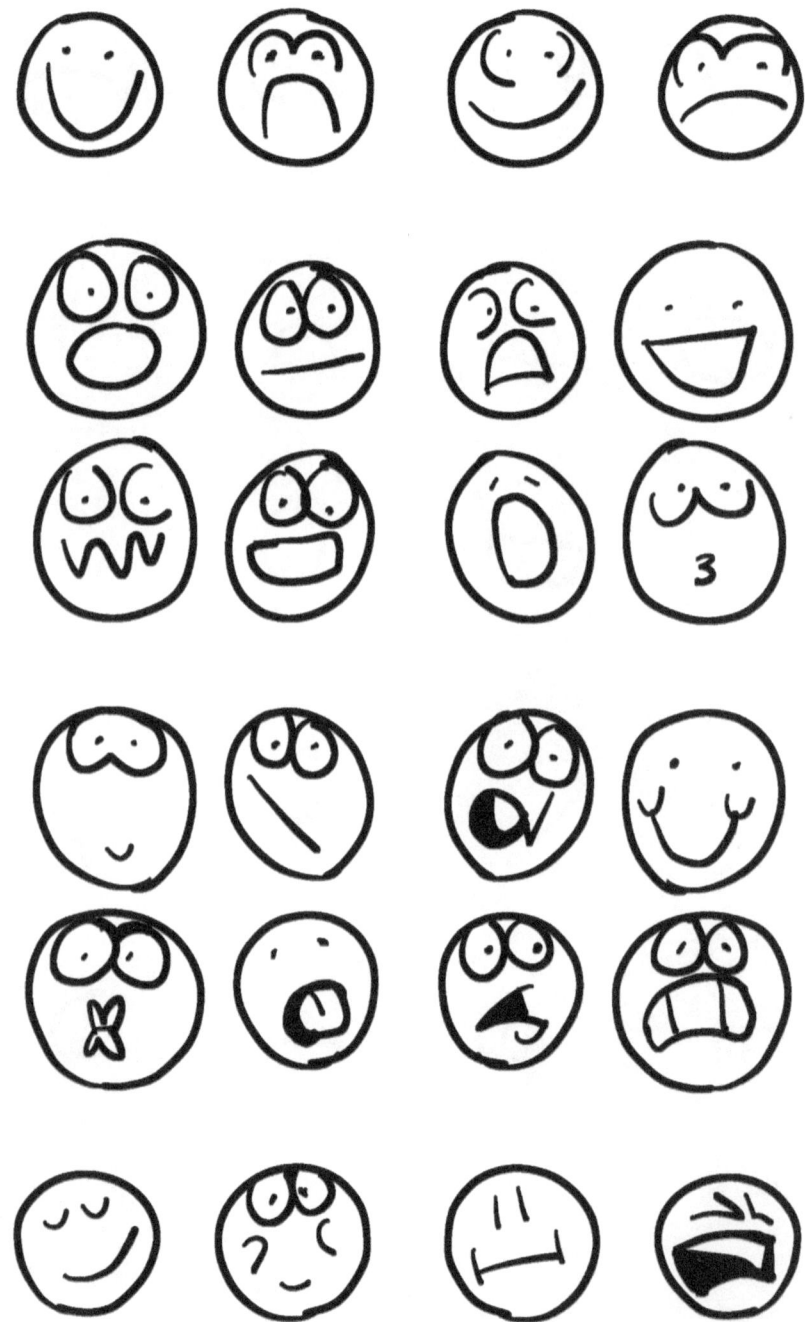

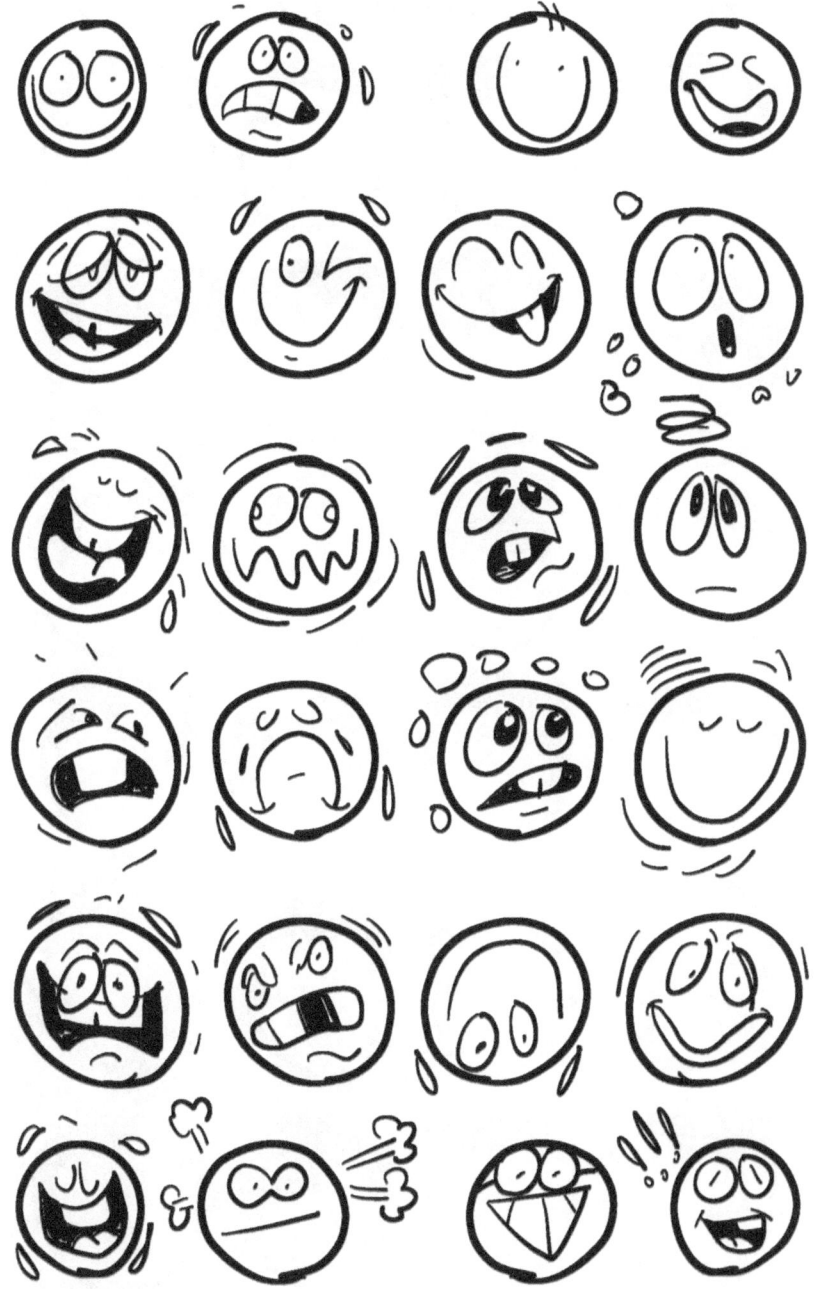

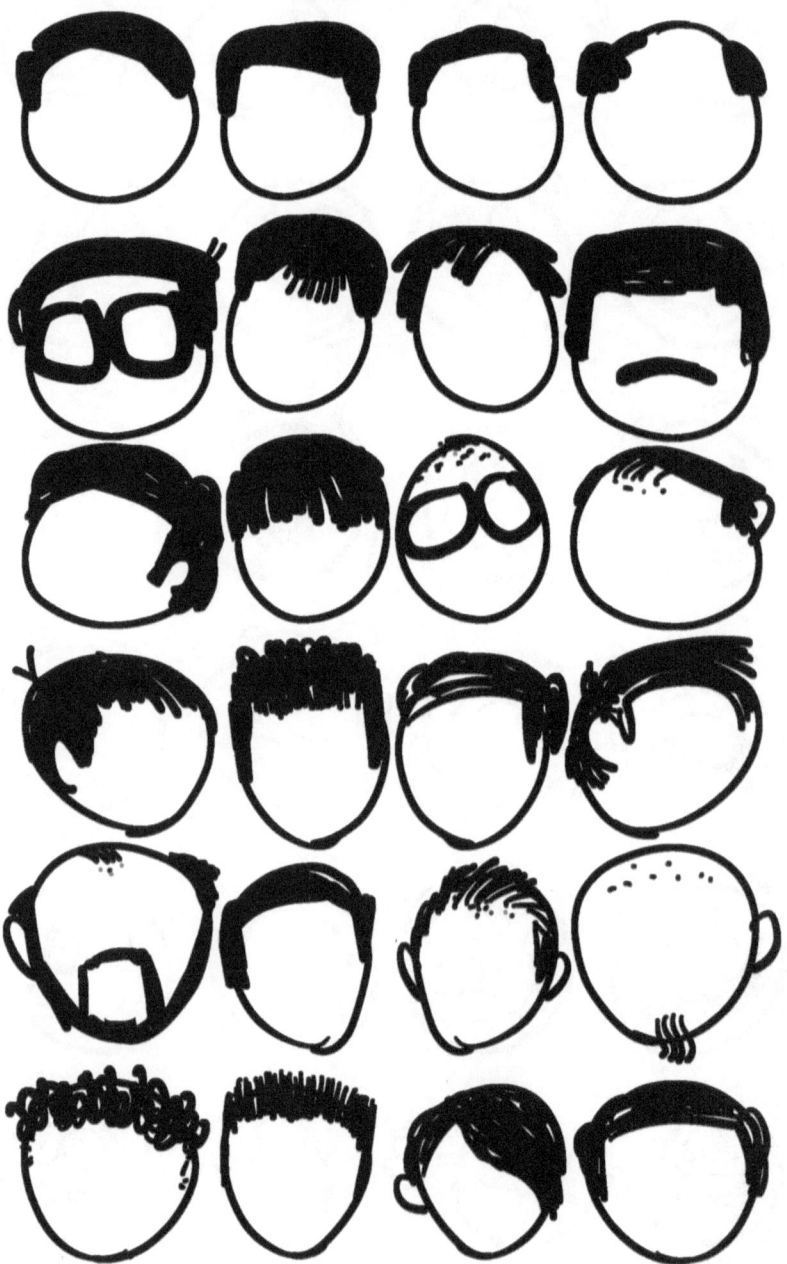

Apply perfect expression on perfect face.

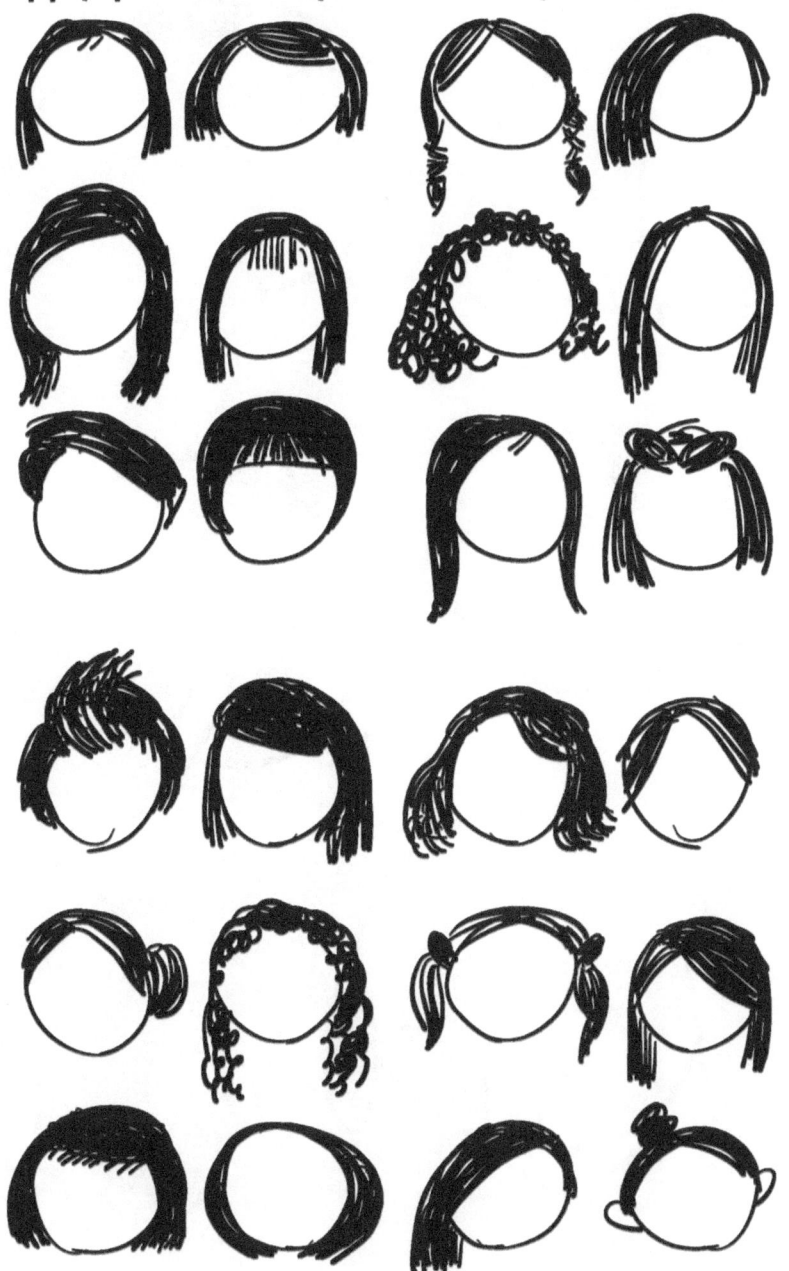

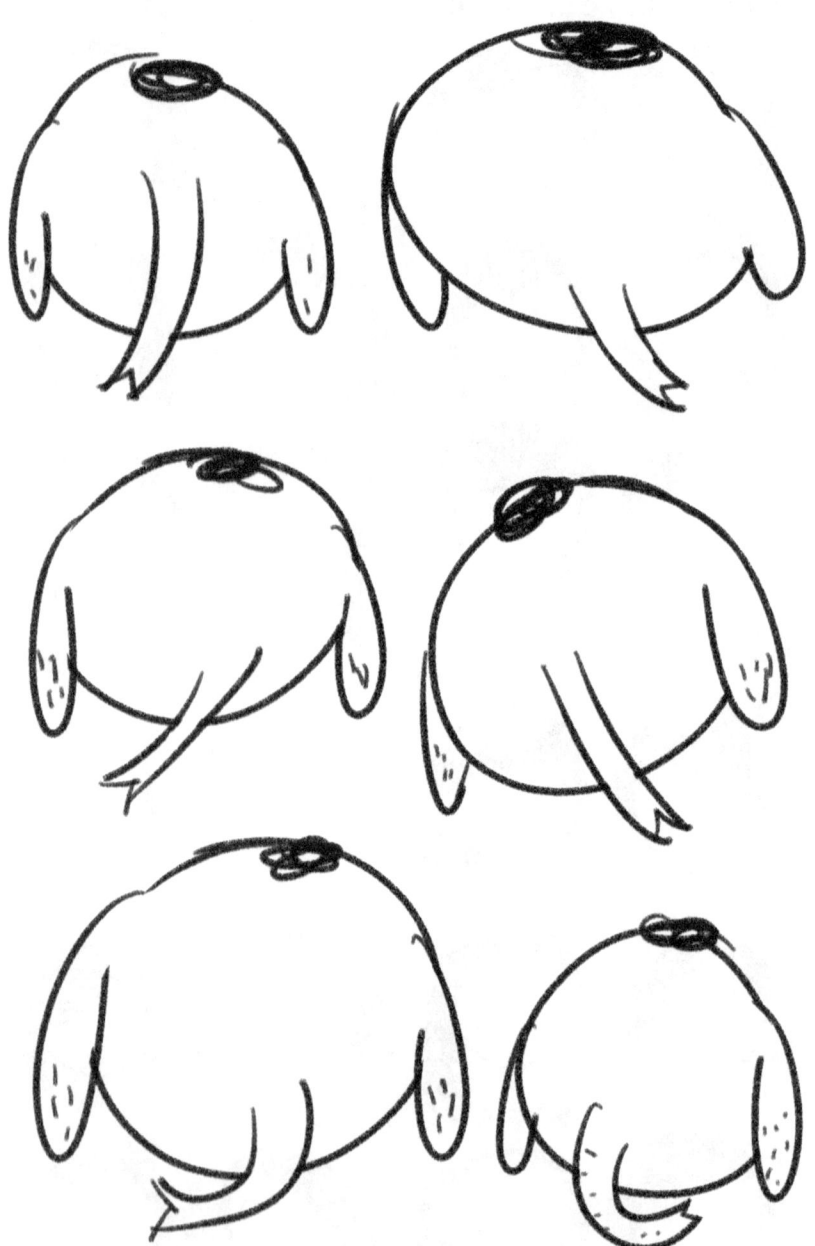

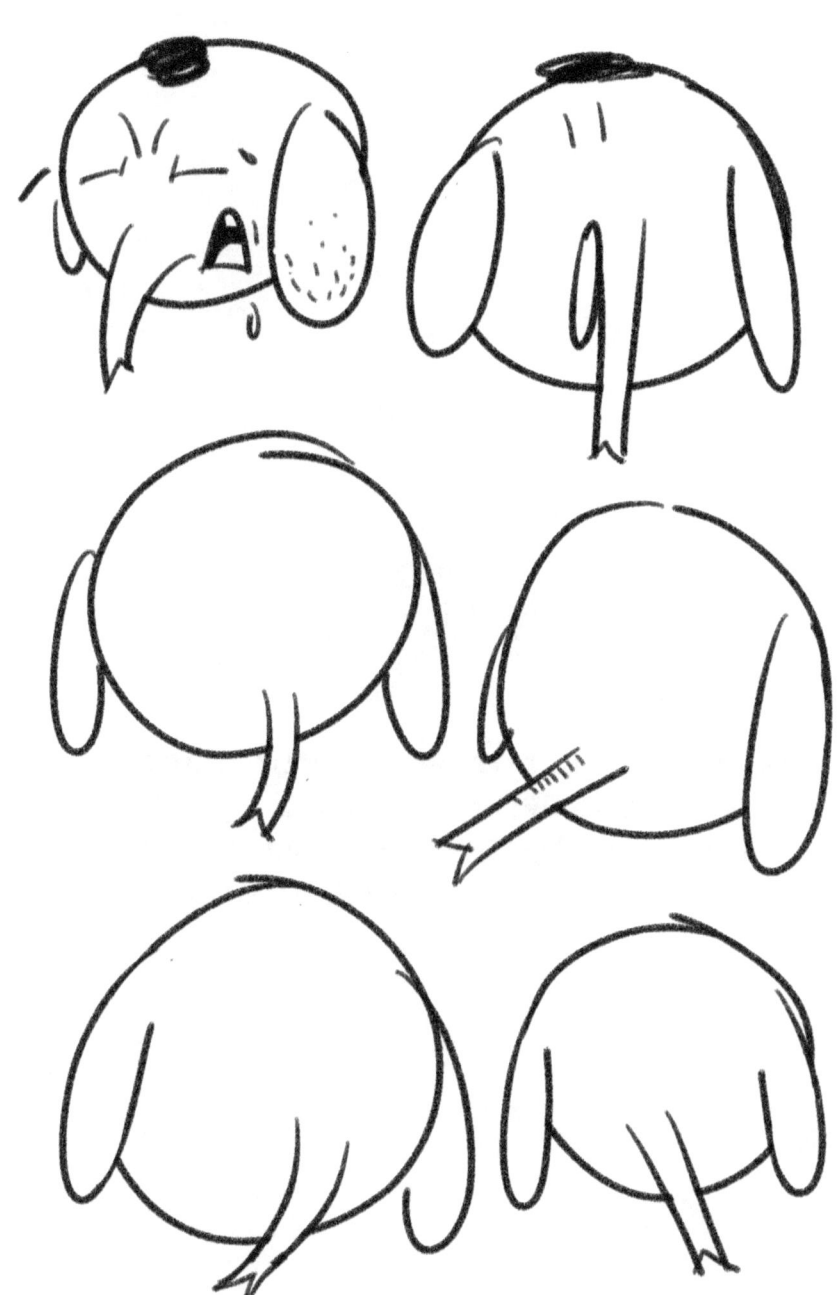

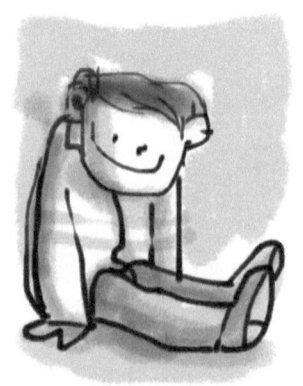

Here is a test to prove your creativity. In this chapter, create a complete character choosing the right hair style, eyes, nose and expression.

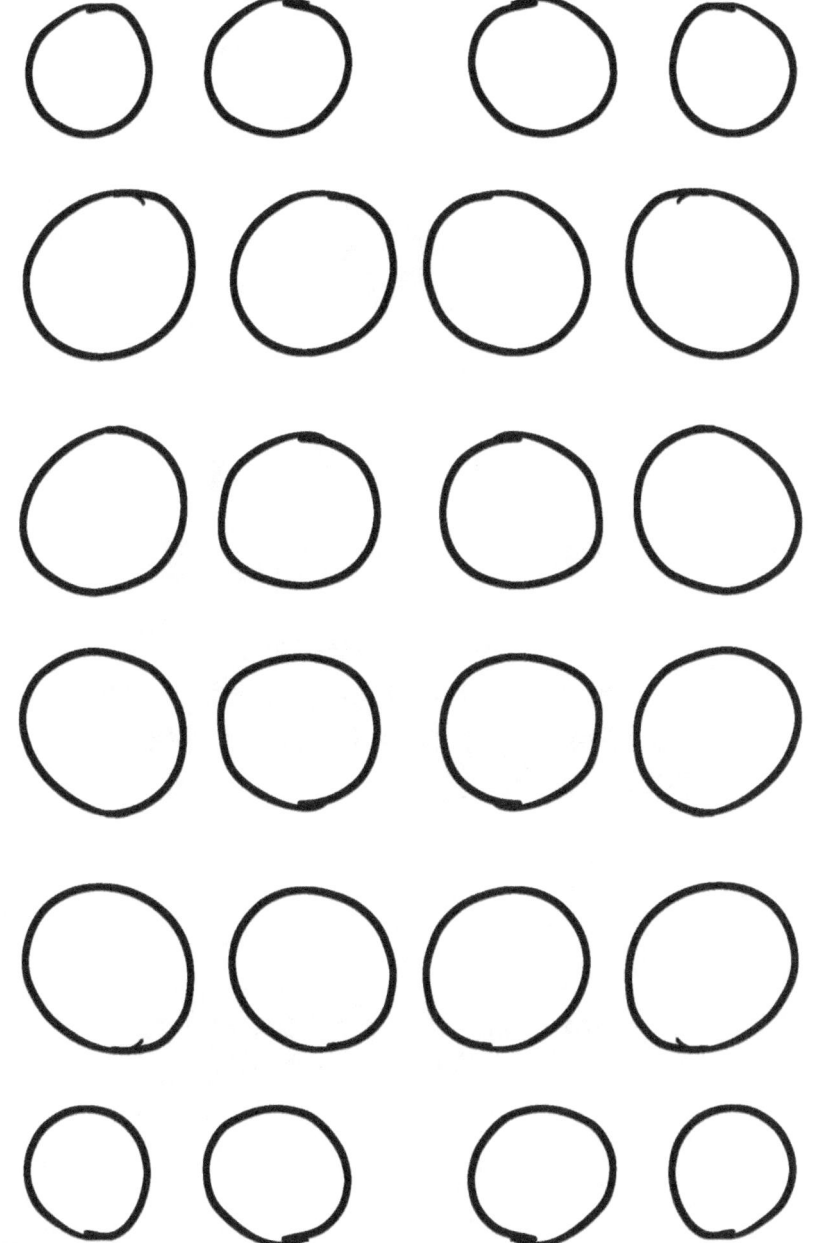

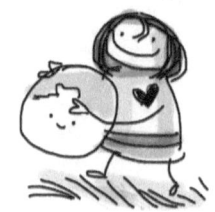

Create your own happiness

Wow! You are awesome!
We are entering a colourful world.
Colouring gives a refreshing feel &
finishing touch to your doodle.

Note: Use colour pencils or
crayons to fill the pages.

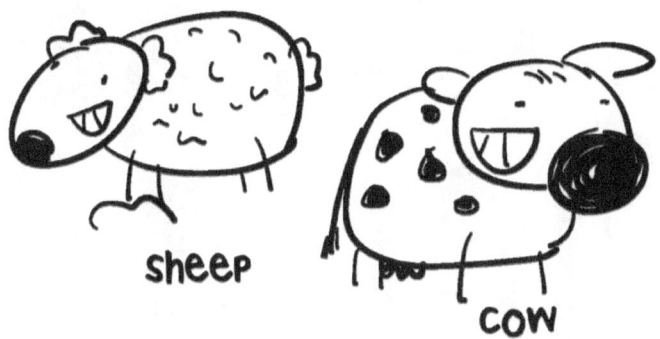
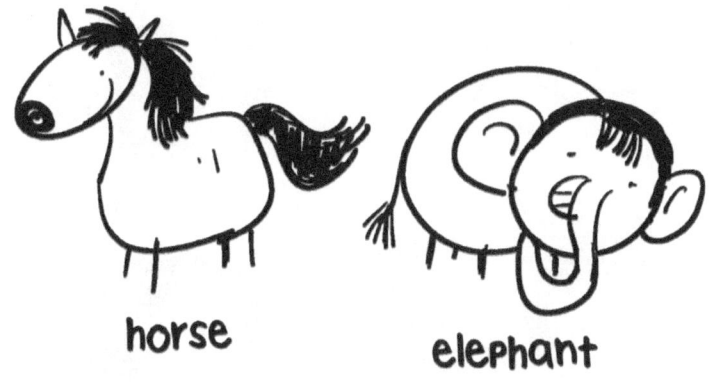
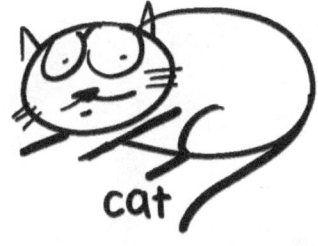
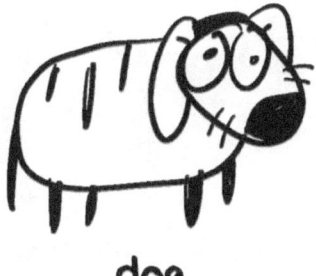

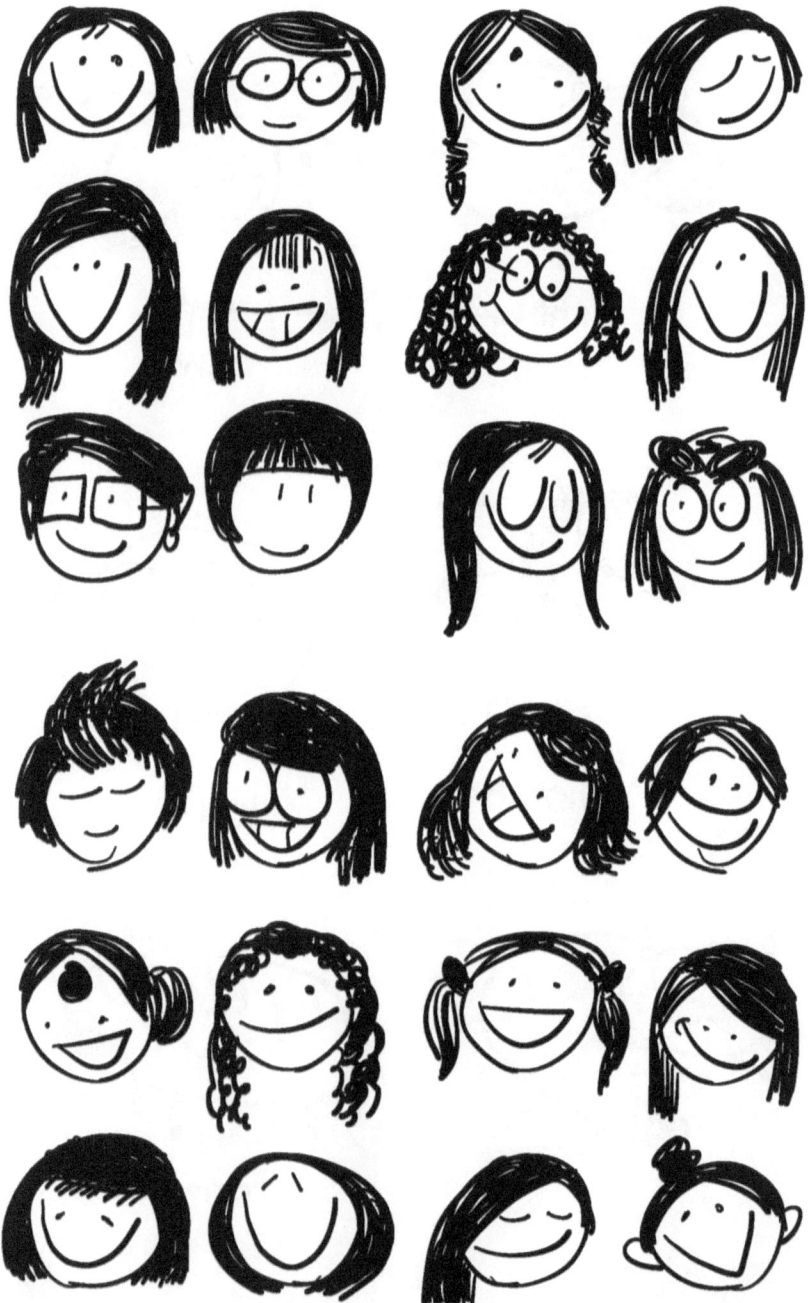

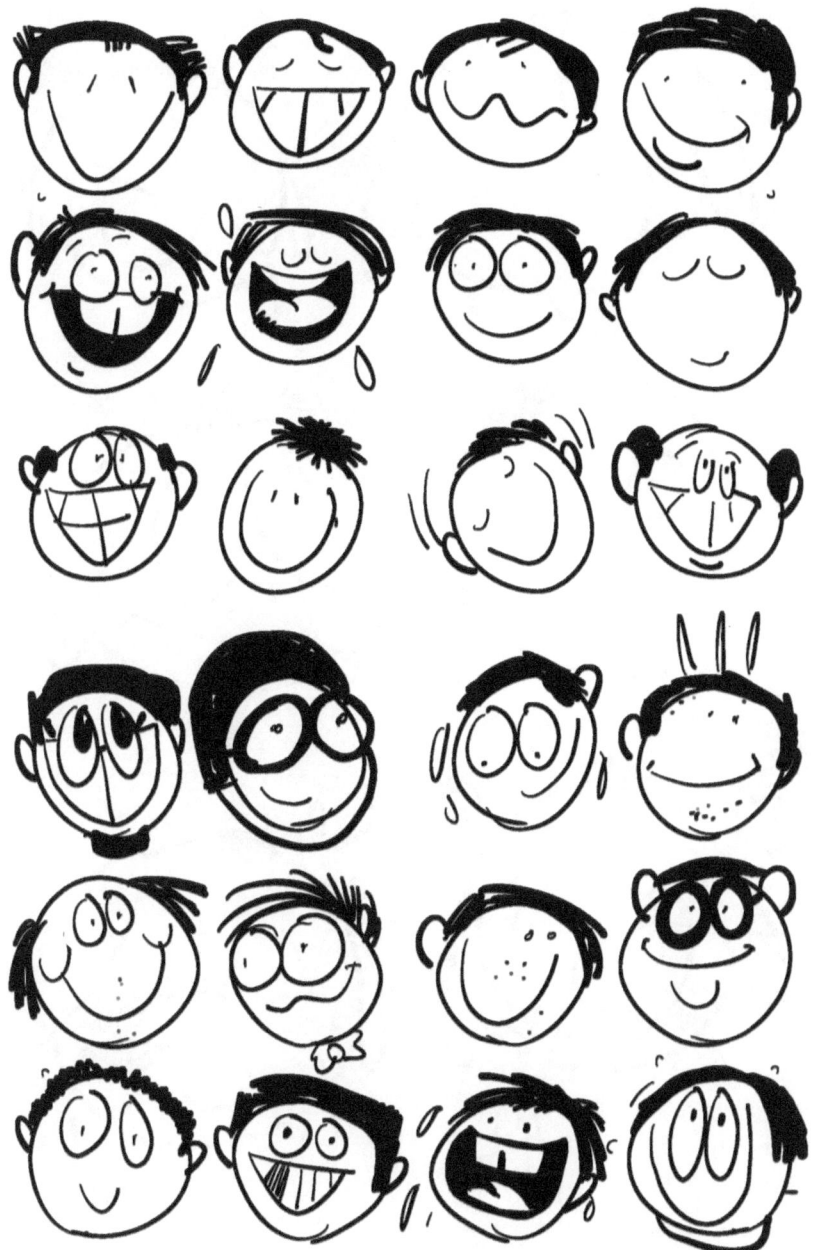

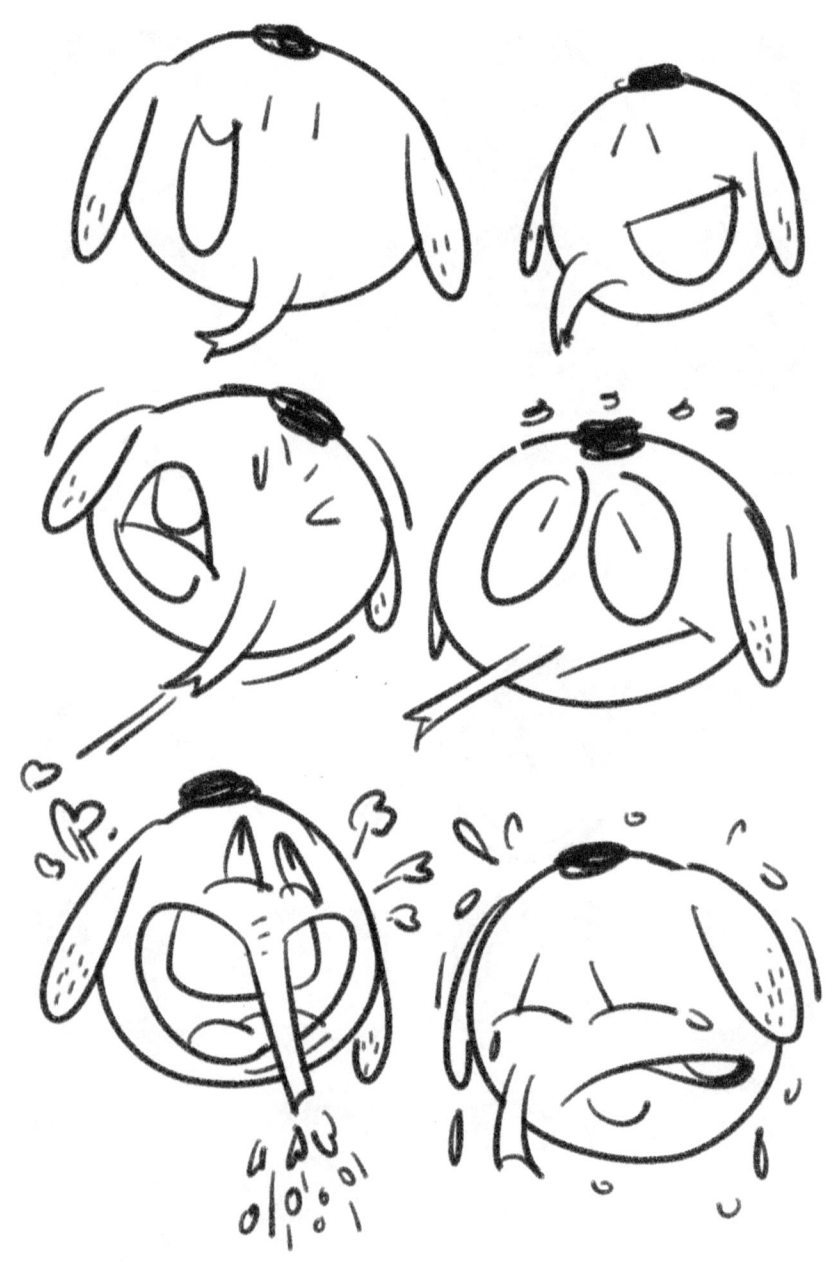

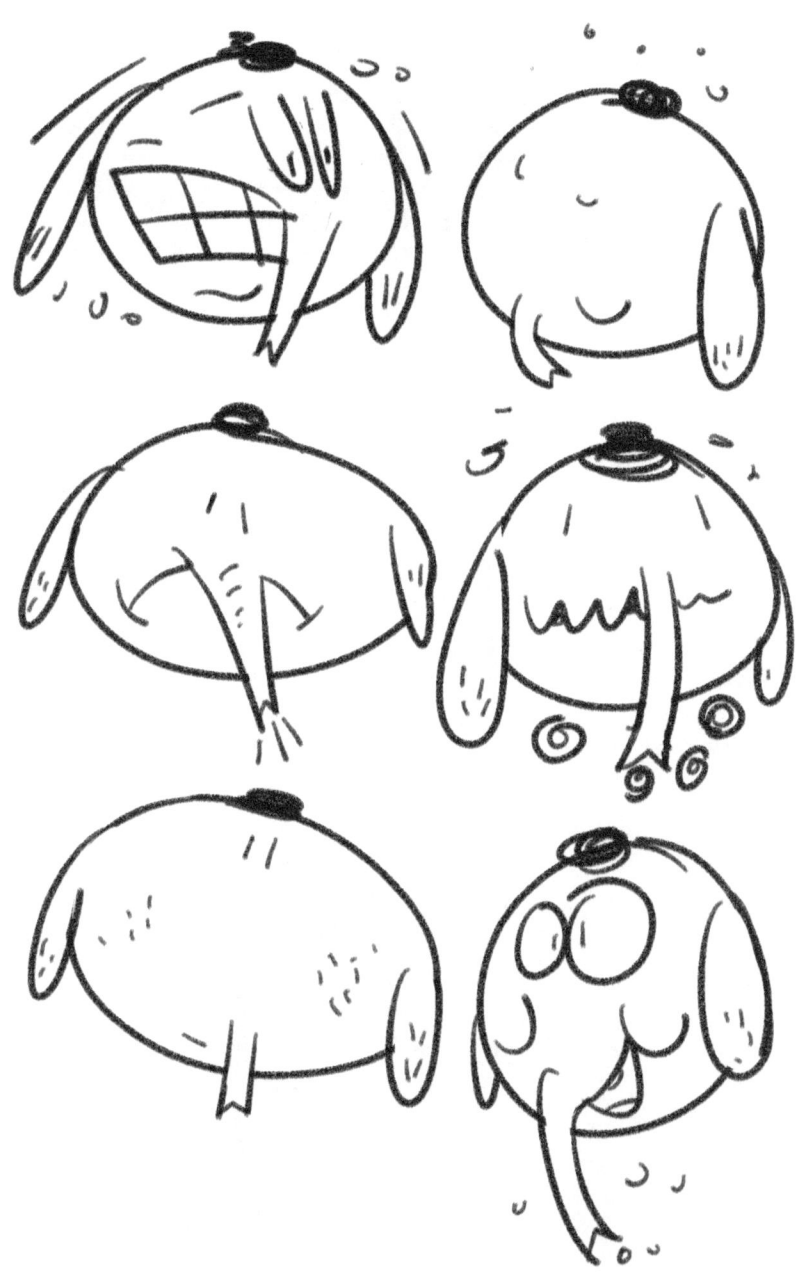

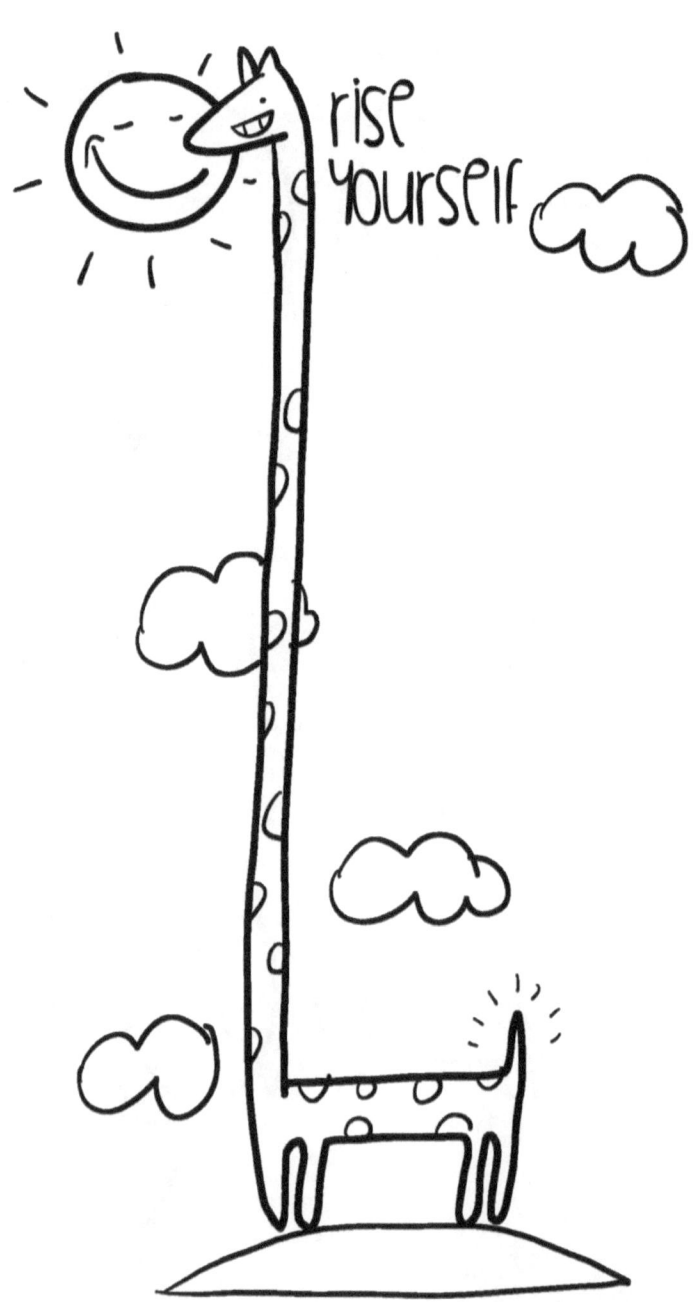

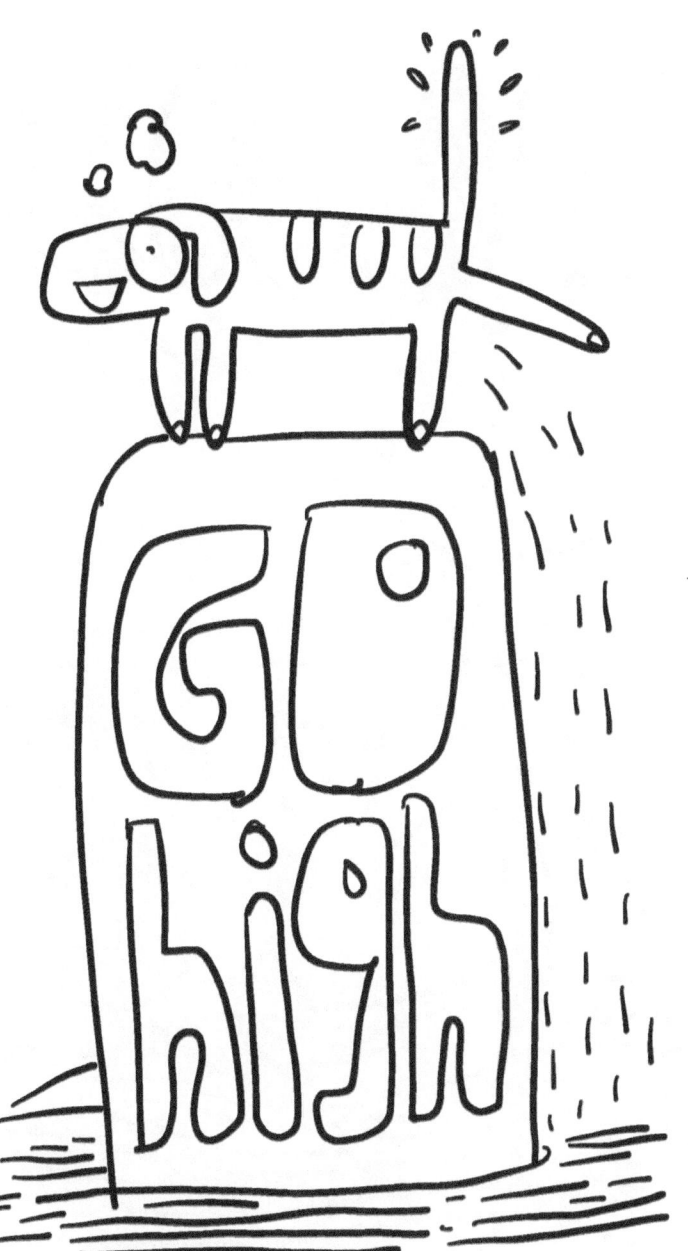

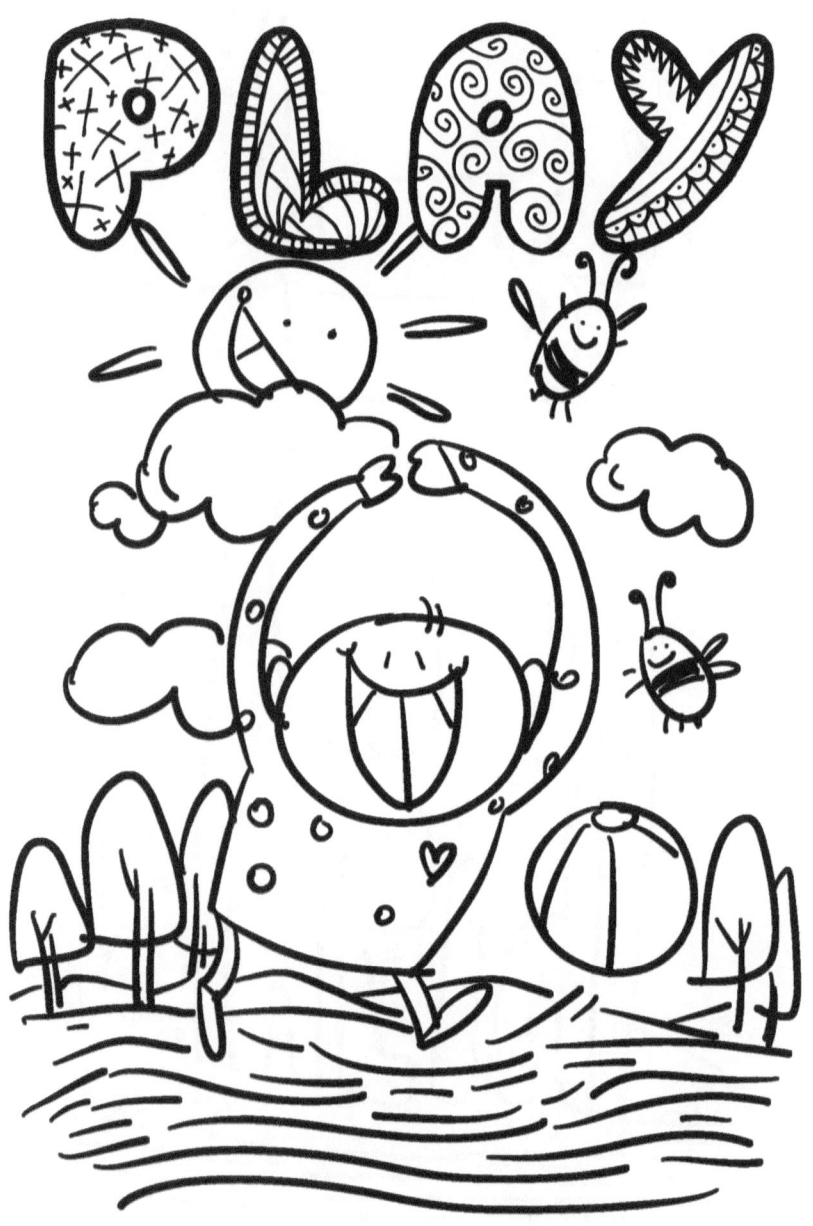

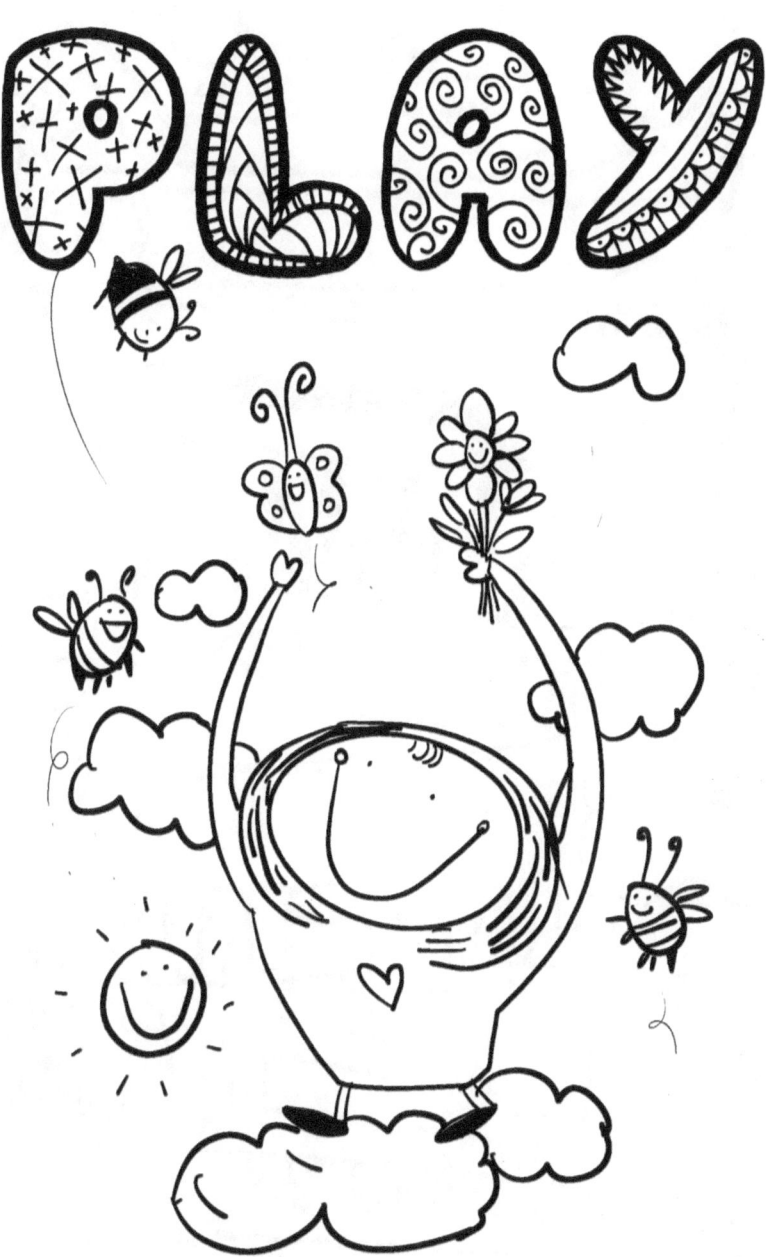

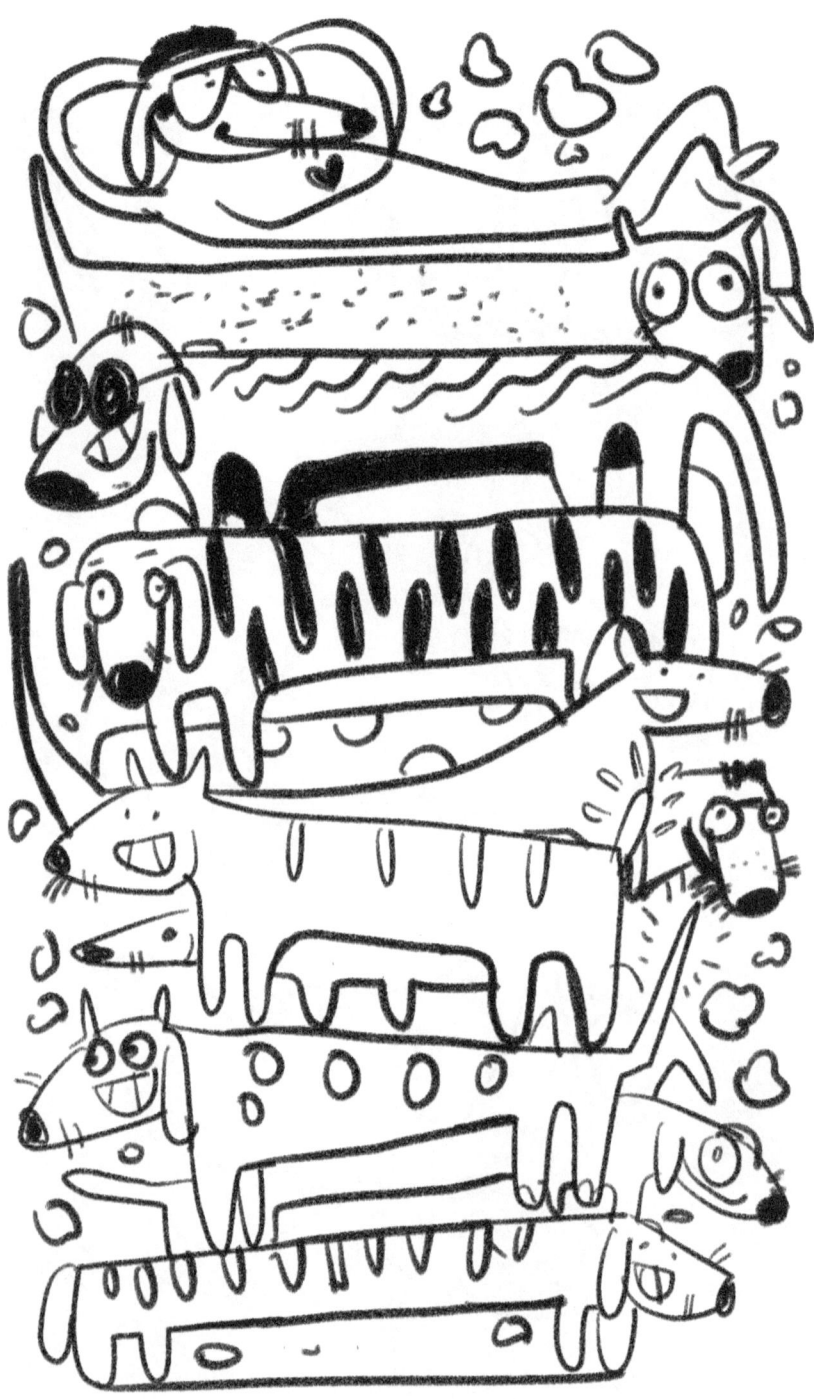

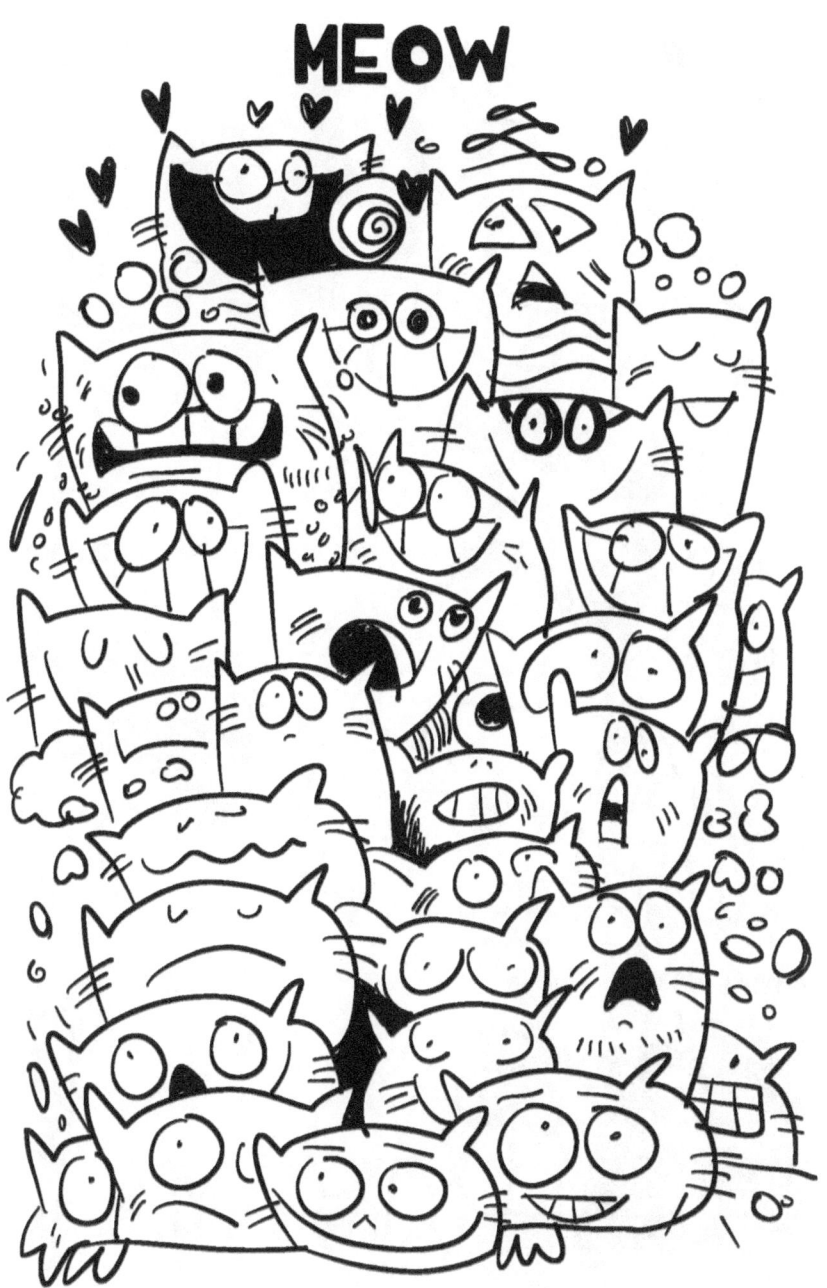

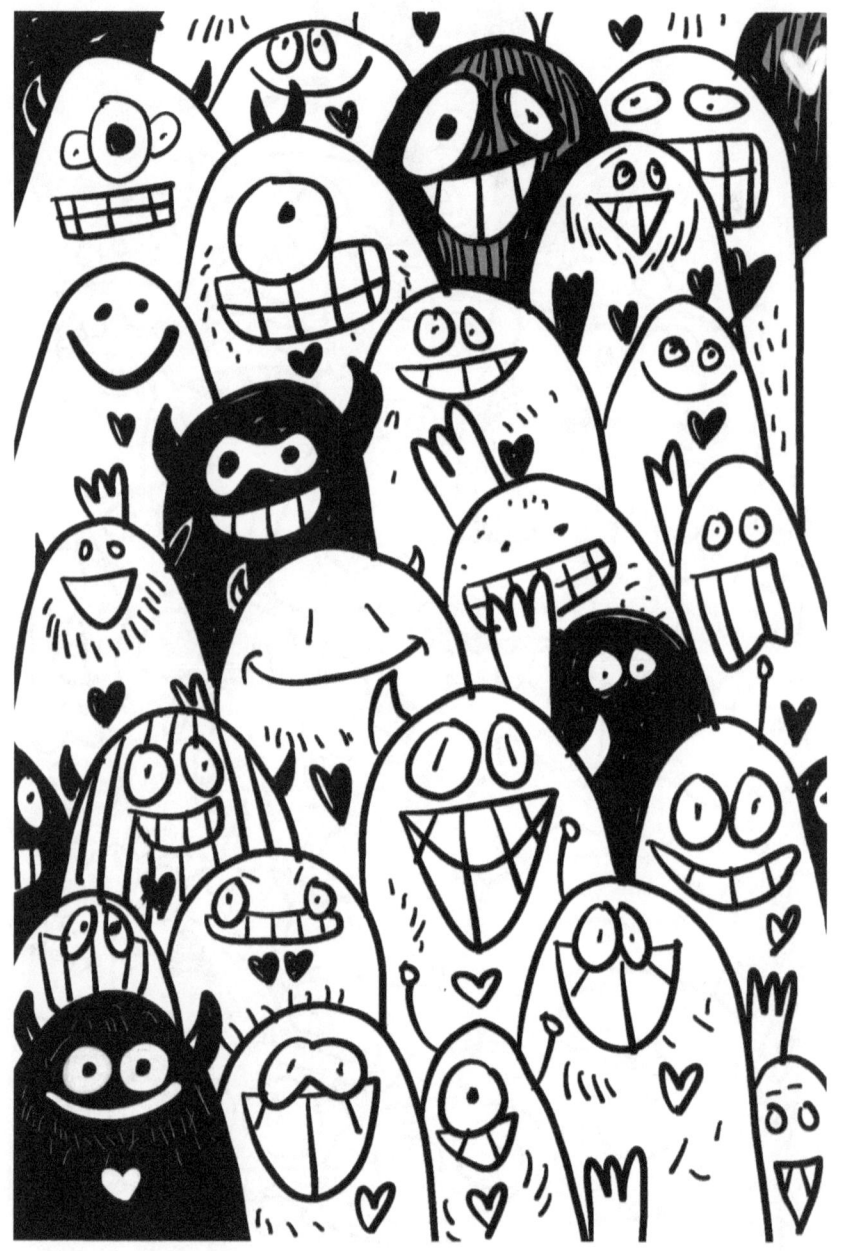

doodle more & color me

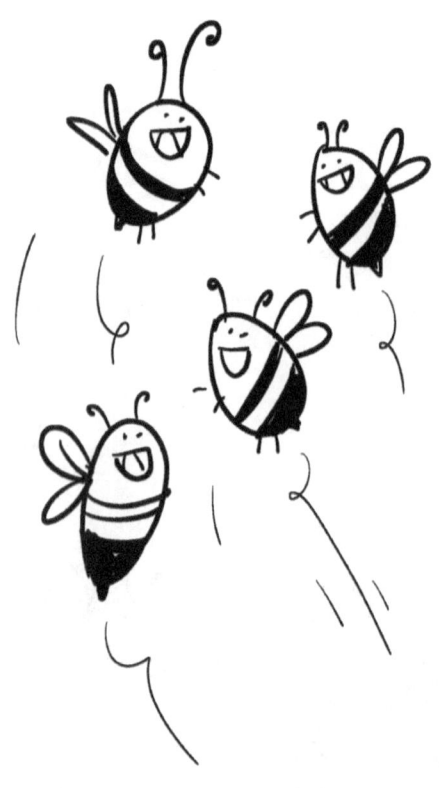

finding happiness in everything

This is an interesting fun activity. There are some scribbled lines on the left side. Use those scribbled lines to create some doodles.

This exercise will boost kids' mental health and enable them to find happiness in everything they do.

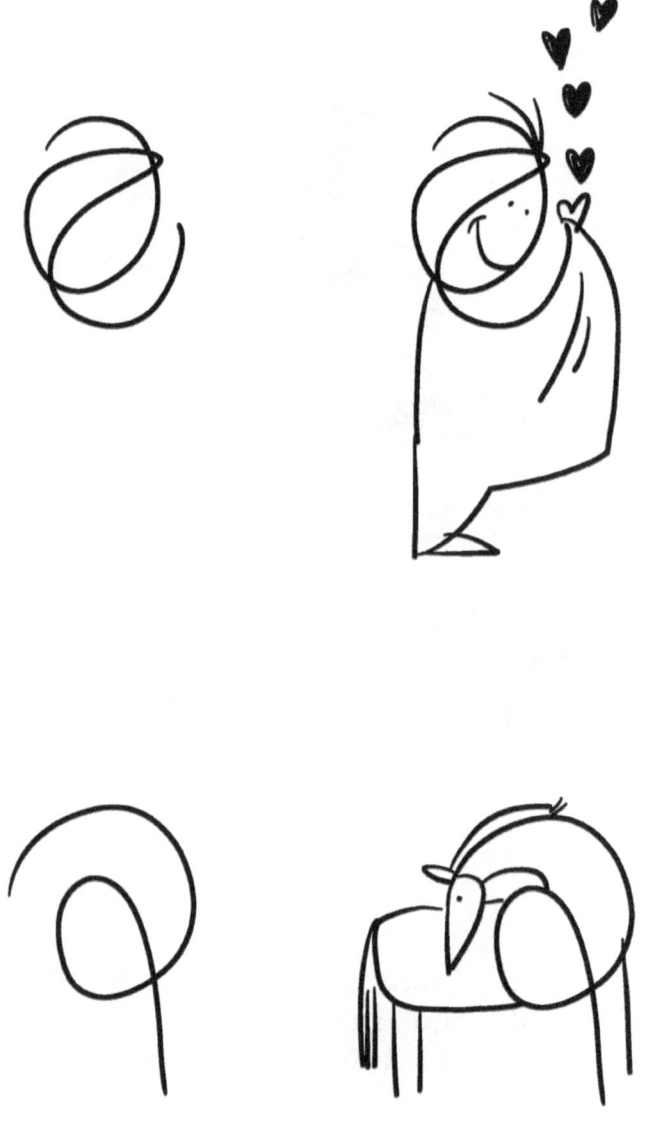

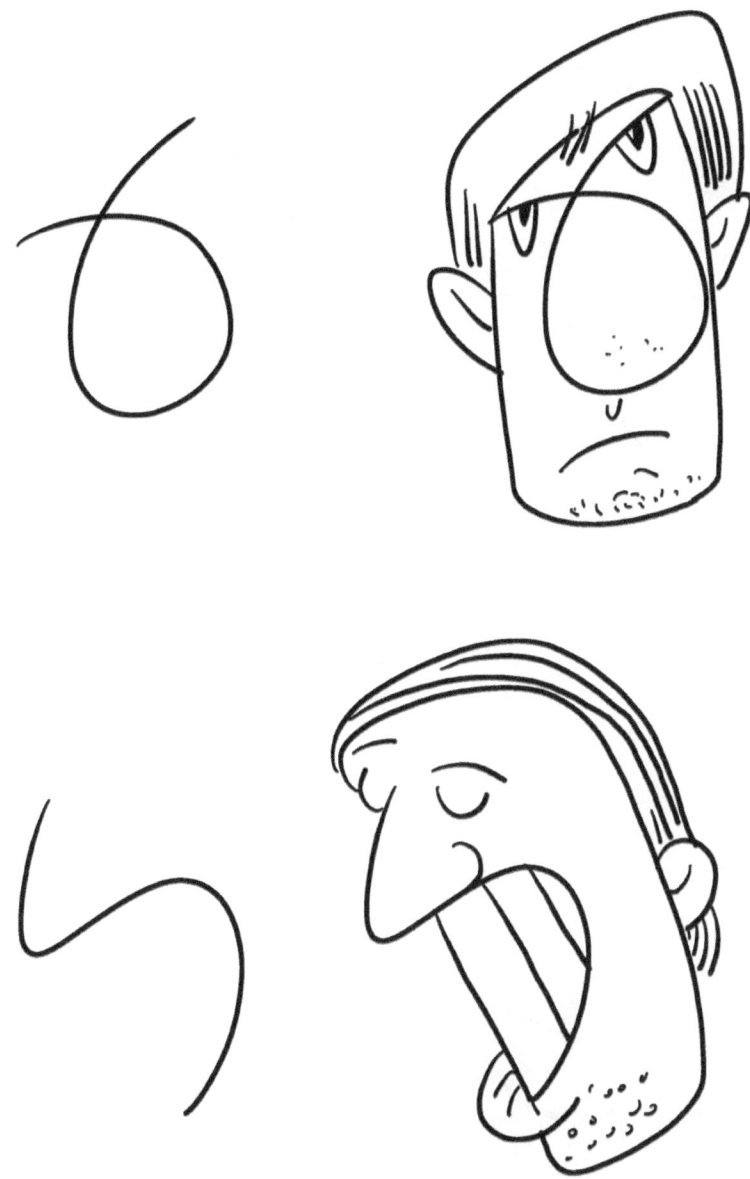

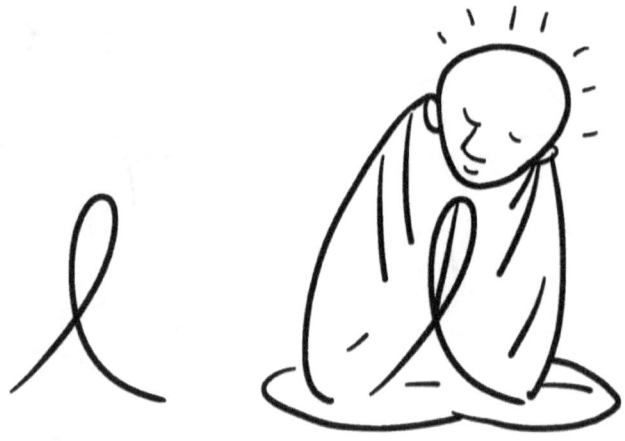

Find yourself

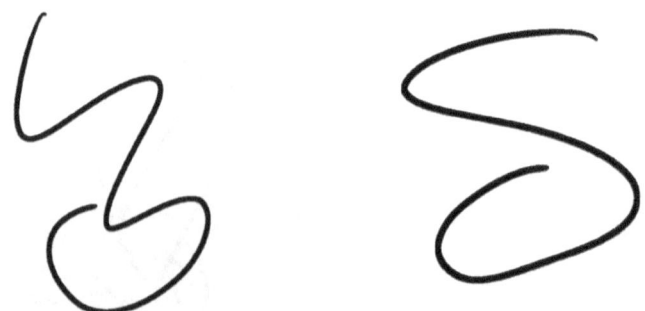

Find yourself

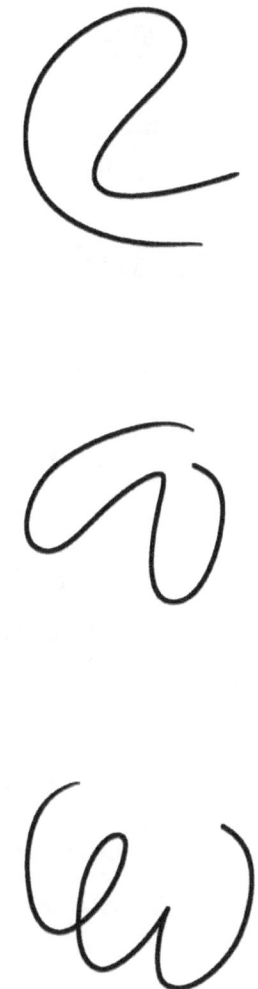

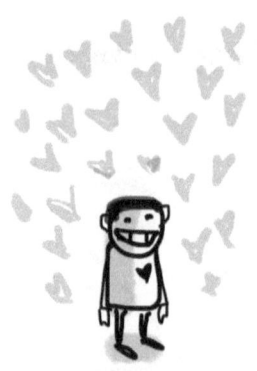

This chapter is full of gratitude doodles.

How to doodle this page?

Create characters with face & expressions. Just think about your father and give him an avatar. Then recollect all the emotions or incidents that you can connect with him and use the full page to express it in doodles. End it by including your note to him in the same page.

Happy Being Family

Characters

Happy man - Your father
Happy woman - Your mother
Happy Kittu - Your Grand Paa
Happy Lattu - Your Grand Maa
Happy Chinu - Your Brother
Happy Jintu - Your Sister
Happy you - Do yourself

Let's spread
#positivevibe

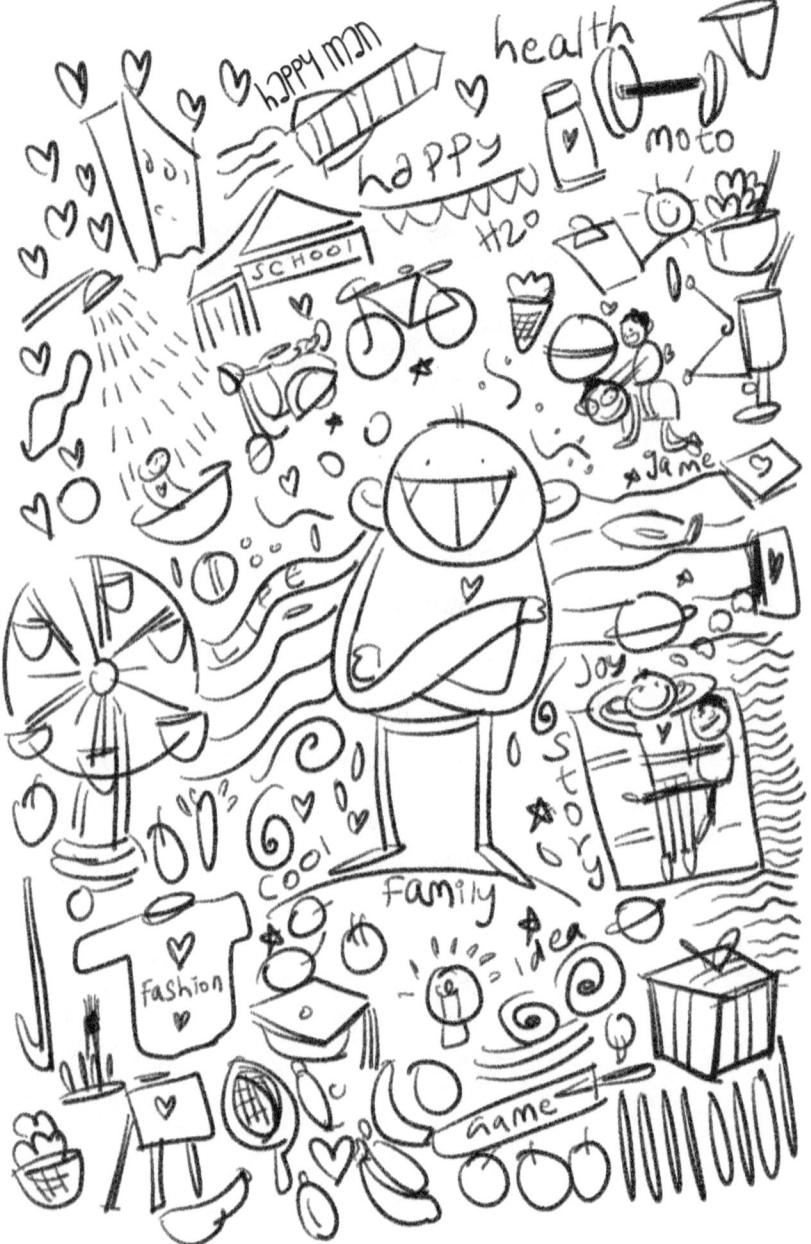

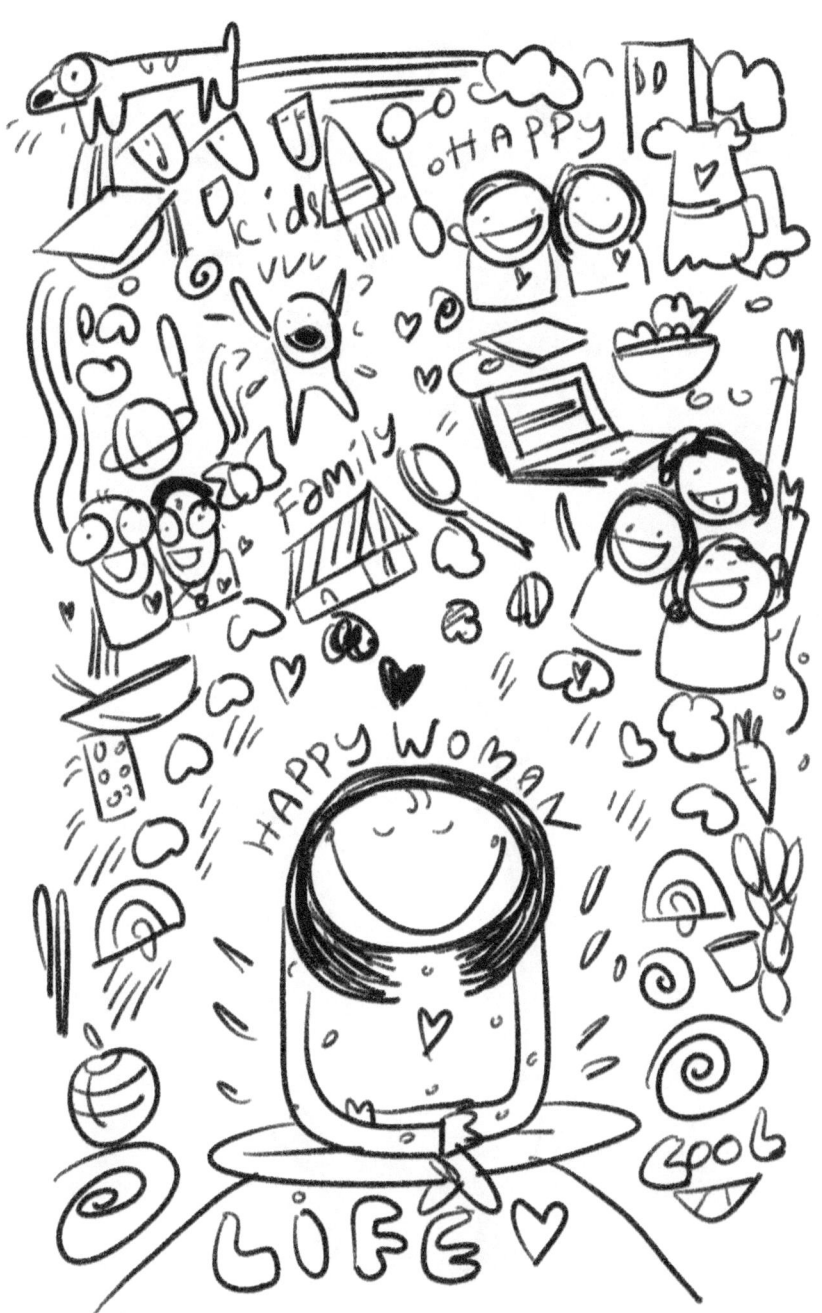

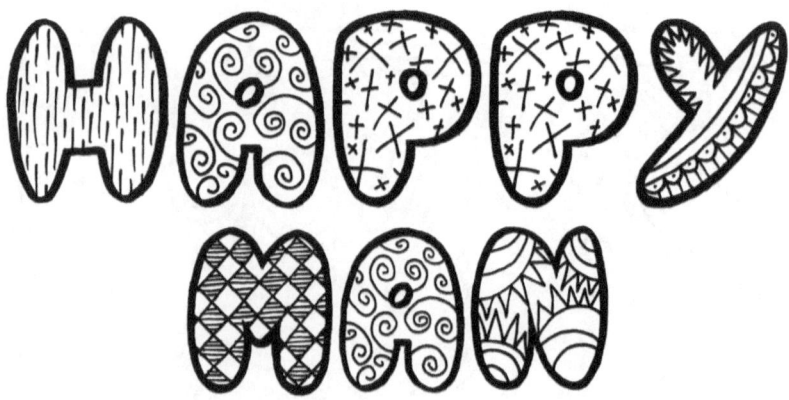
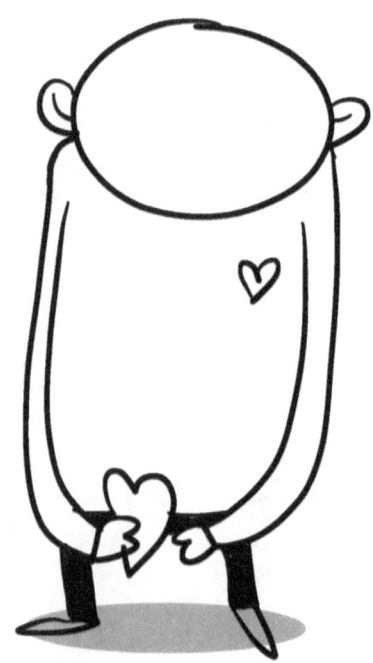

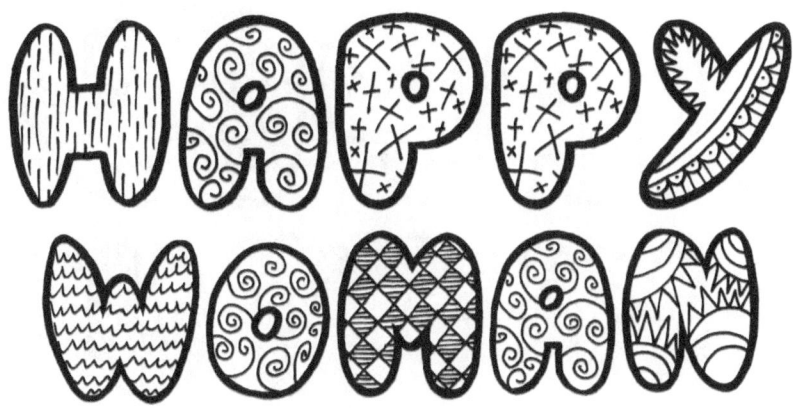
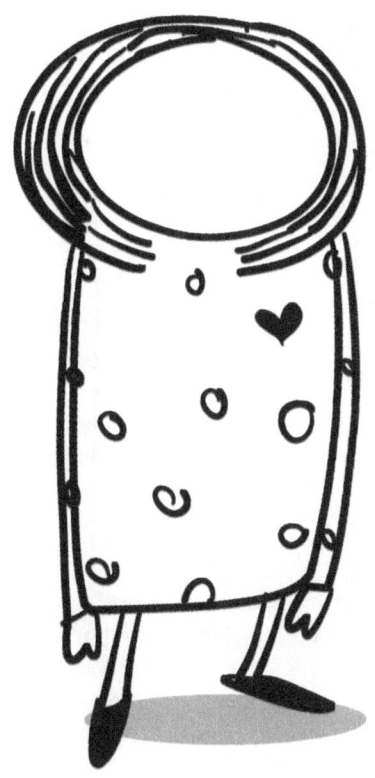

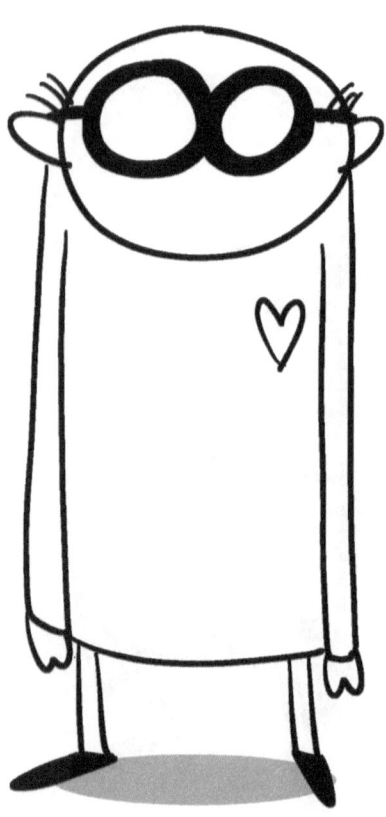

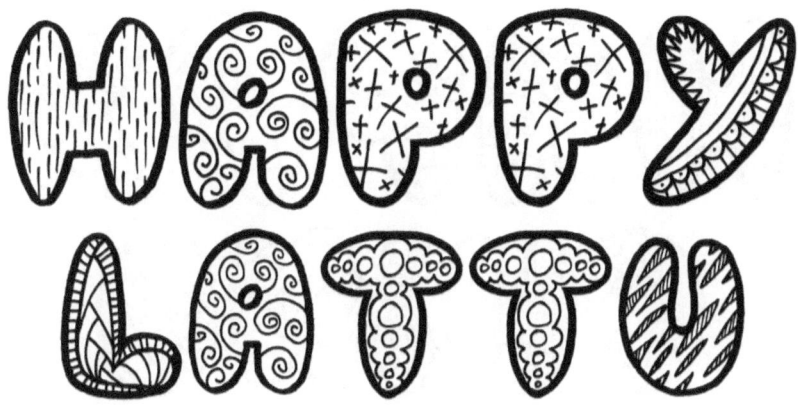
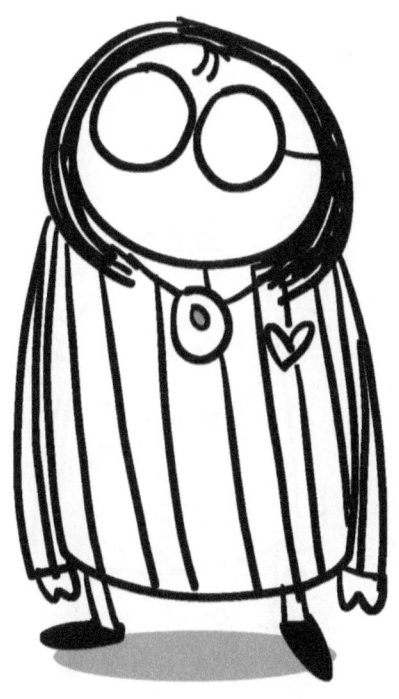

HAPPY CHINU

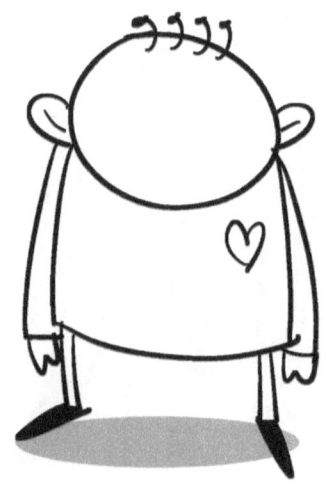

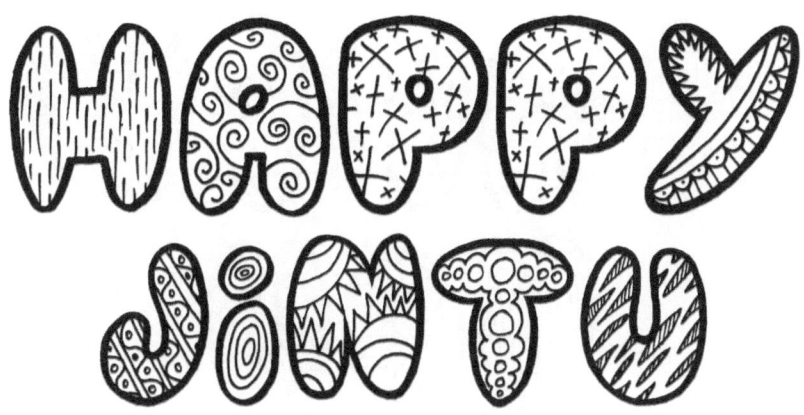

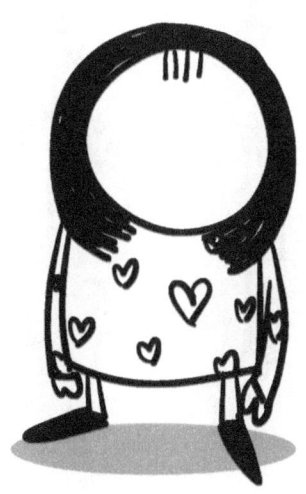

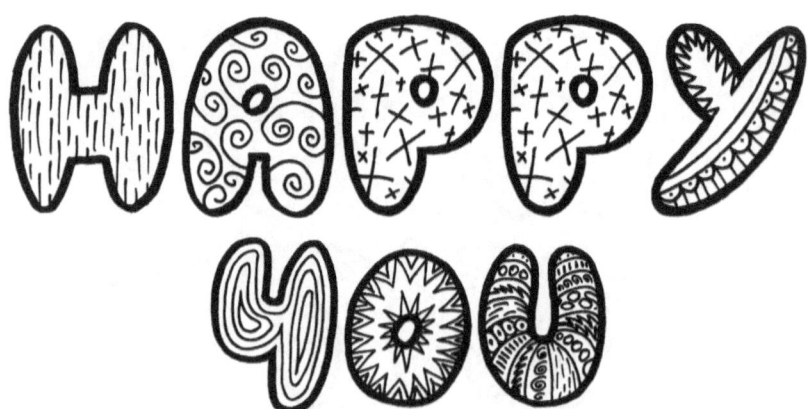
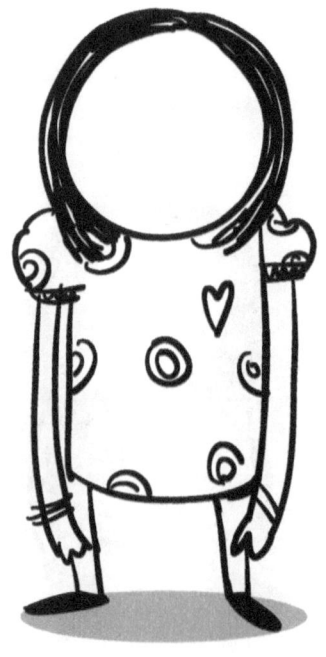

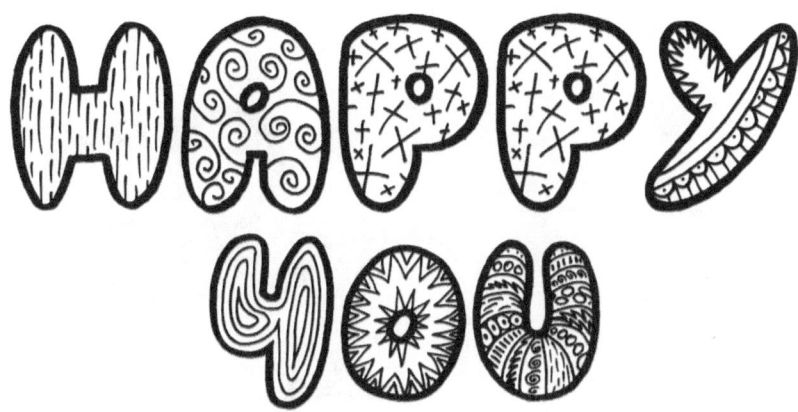

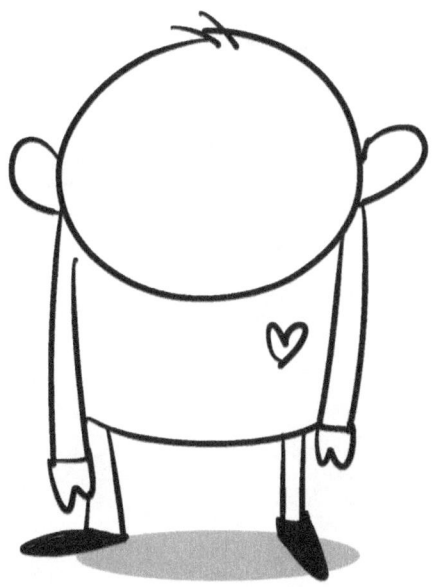

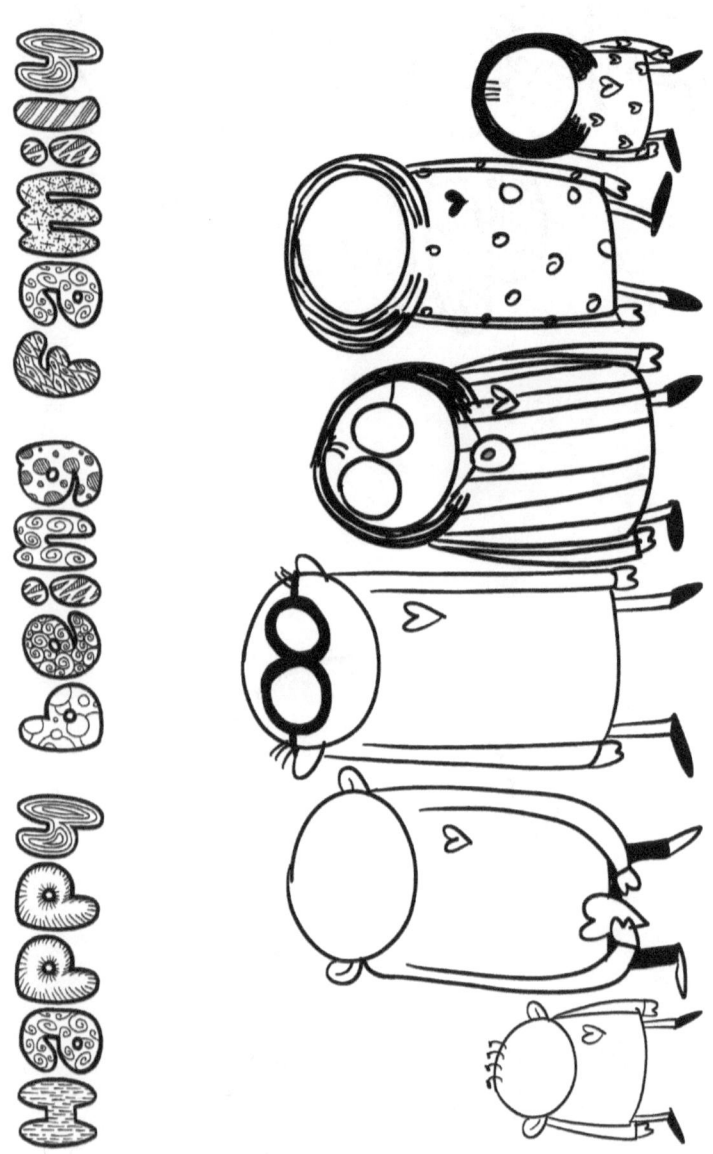

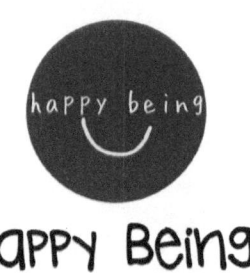

Happy Being

Simple things bring happiness to our lives
Happy Being is one among us.
Happy Being Family
finds happiness in small things.
Happy Man, Happy Woman, Happy Lala, Lily, Lali,
Chinu, Jintu, Kittu & Lattu.
give u the daily dose of happiness
to kick start ur day with loads offer enthusiasm.
Happy Being brings out
the hidden happiness in life.

Happiness is all about how we approach life.

Happy Being for Being Happy

#spreadlove

follow us

www.happybeingdoodles.com

www.ingramcontent.com/pod-product-compliance
Lightning Source LLC
Chambersburg PA
CBHW030509220526
45464CB00006B/2726